# THE NEW RUSSIA

# THE NEW RUSSIA

## Communism in Evolution

edited by **Denis Dirscherl, S.J.**

Pflaum Press  Dayton, Ohio   1968

First Printing, 1968
Copyright: © 1968 by Pflaum Press
Library of Congress Catalog Card Number: 68-21350
Printed in the United States of America

# Introduction

---

Few major political, religious or social movements in history have been able to survive and maintain the enthusiasm and fervor of their early years. Many, indeed, attacked from the outside or subjected to internal decay, eventually lose their vitality, disintegrate and slip from the memory of mankind. Despite some of the inevitable forces of ruin, one of history's most colossal and world-shaking movements continues to survive and preserve a surprising measure of its pristine inner fiber and strength, however different in character some of its aspects may be from their origins. Soviet Russia, the showcase of international communism, has managed to maintain its own inner dynamic in spite of having reached a stage wherein most of those men who had a part in the Revolution of 1917 and the events of the following decade either are now dead or no longer exert a strong influence in the country's affairs.

Today, after over fifty years of Soviet rule, there is a new Russia. A new image, and, more importantly, a new reality are emerging from the country that Sir Winston Churchill once described as "a riddle wrapped in a mystery inside an enigma." Prerevolutionary Russia was one of the least well-known of the major European countries. And the Soviets' early unwillingness to communicate with the world compelled most nations to remain in almost total ignorance of many internal conditions and policy intentions of the new regime. Soviet censorship and restrictions all but stymied the concern and curiosity of the West to know what was taking place in a seemingly chaotic Russia. Only within the past decade or so has the West really been able to pierce the Iron Curtain. Especially since the Twentieth Party Congress in 1956, which included N. S. Khrushchev's denunciation of Stalin, the barrier has lifted enough to allow the West to penetrate the personalities and changing structures of Soviet society. Because the West is now better informed of actualities in Russia, the world is that much more secure and able to deal with the growing complexities of international confrontations at all levels. Most noteworthy of all, the growing desire for an increasing interchange of ideas reflects the pressures for freedom and peace that are mounting in the middle of the twentieth century, a heartening fact that can all too easily be overlooked in an era of crisis fixations.

More realistic appraisals of the "giants of the 'sixties" like Russia will insure a safer and saner world. This volume, then, hopes to be a modest contribution to the ongoing analyses of Russia and international communism. What changes are taking place in Russia today? What are her problems, and how does she attempt to resolve them? What are her achievements? What are the important constants among all the variables? In short, whither Russia? These are the large questions that ten carefully chosen specialists in the field of Russian studies have undertaken to probe in this book. Centering chiefly on the post-Stalin period leading up to the present, all the crucial categories of Soviet life, thought and action are considered: agriculture, domestic politics, economics, education, international affairs, the literary scene, the military, philosophy, religion and youth.

Professor Richard Mills of Fordham University begins our study with his chapter on "Issues and Leadership in Soviet Politics" in which he deals with some of the major intricacies of the Soviet ruling apparatus. As he indicates, Russia is a country where greater pluralism is in the making and old structures are found inadequate to face the new needs of the citizenry and complexities of internal politics. New voices for consensus agreement are making their influence felt. Professor Mills deftly handles the problems surrounding the "cult of the personality," the unequal balance of power among the factions seeking control in Russia, and the changing structures of government. In his analysis there is room for a guarded optimism: "The Soviet Union is still in a very delicate stage of transition from dictatorship to a more representative form of government."

Moving to another area of paramount concern to Soviet planners, Professor Arthur Wright of Oberlin College explores the economic scene, focusing on five critical areas that often appear to be nothing more than a bewildering mass of jumbled facts and figures. In the context of the new breed of technocrats and engineers who are gaining more of a voice in policy-making, and of the rapid changes which call for constant expert attention and adaptation, Professor Wright analyzes some key areas of constant frustration to Soviet economists: problems in growth rates, repeated failures in agriculture including the "virgin lands" project, the tension between "guns and butter," and the overall problem of the demand for decentralization. The more flexible policies in economic planning as advocated by men such as Y. G. Liberman, and the whetted appetites of Soviet citizenry for the good things of life, Professor Wright points out, will almost certainly call for more revamping of the economic structure of Soviet society.

A specialist in Soviet agriculture, Professor Roy Laird of the University of Kansas, devotes his attention to current policies on the Soviet collective farms. He writes, "The collectivized agricultural system is, perhaps, the most important of all of Stalin's questionable gifts to the Soviet system of rule; certainly it is the overriding feature of the Soviet rural scene." Indeed, the influence of agriculture on the entire Soviet economy cannot be overemphasized. Despite the fact, however, that chronic problems on the majority of collectives call for major reforms, party officials are still slow to show a willingness to face their difficulties directly. Professor Laird closes his study with the conclusion that effective changes on the farm front will not be implemented until party officials see that the system, and not just the management and leadership, is faulty.

Mr. William Jackson of the Institute for International Youth Affairs in New York examines the youth question in his chapter on the "Young Soviets and an Aging *Komsomol*." This sector of Soviet society is highly significant. As Mr. Jackson points out, over half the Soviet population is under twenty-six years of age. What the Soviet Union will become in the very near future will depend on her young people. Presently, the gap—one might say chasm—between the younger and older generations is deep. In times past there is no question that the Communist party and its ideological and educational policies effectively harnessed the energies and enthusiasm of youth for the government's purposes. Today this is no longer true. Time and again we hear in the Soviet press of disgruntled youth who are weary of the "Party line" and avid for truth. Repeated efforts to instill greater ideological fervor are of little avail. Mr. Jackson presents a well rounded approach for understanding the attitudes and tensions of youth vis-à-vis the present power structure.

Shifting to the field of education, Dr. Nicholas DeWitt of Indiana University, contributes a chapter on "Recent Changes in Soviet Educational Policy." In his prospectus of the Soviet educational system he carefully delineates the difficulties of a comparatively monistic concept of educational planning with its inadequate short-term solutions to long-range problems. Though Soviet educational reforms have failed to produce the widely heralded "new Soviet man," they have made great strides forward since the beginning of the Revolution. Few countries can match the Soviet achievement in this regard. But as Professor DeWitt writes, "The Soviet individual and the Soviet State are engaged in a highly pragmatic game—who gets what out of whom." The student still finds his future defined in terms of serving the State.

The role of philosophy in Soviet society normally receives attention only in highly technical journals. Today, however, the official ideology that was once considered almost monolithic and incapable of change reveals the pressures of the times; it is on the defensive. Soviet orthodoxy, so powerful in the past, has become stultified and removed further and further from reality through years of mere repetition with little interest in "updating" Marxism-Leninism. Professor James Scanlan of Goucher College puts this puzzle into focus. The Soviets themselves, he points out, realize that other points of view have merit, and this is manifested in many ways. "Disagreement and discussion are less feared," he writes, than in the past, and if present conditions persist, Russia is headed for a much more open society. To this date interest far outstrips available information about conditions outside Russia, but it seems inevitable that this situation will change more as the government is moved to soften its hold over censorship of the foreign mass media.

The literary scene is often a thermometer of reaction in the

Soviet Union. The ferment, the various tugs-of-war between liberal and conservative factions, is most obvious in this important realm of Soviet life. Timothy McClure assesses the ups and downs of these political pressures in his chapter on the cultural front. Incidents like the trials of Andrei Siniavski and Yuli Daniel not only demonstrate the heavy hand the Party still holds over the Union of Soviet Writers but also indicate that a still long and painful process lies ahead before freedom of expression is won in the Soviet Union. The "system" is destined to create yet more alienated intellectuals. Included in Mr. McClure's chapter is his "Digression on Labels," a handy guideline to the various trends and personalities in Soviet literature.

One of the most difficult subjects in Russian studies to assess realistically is the question of religion. For years now, the situation there has been described as the "Church in chains," or the "Church of silence." The subject is complicated by the absence of a cross section of information based on scientific investigations. Dr. Paul B. Anderson, consultant to the National Council of Churches in New York, tackles this difficult topic. One conclusion from his study supports the general contention that the practice of a formal, institutionalized religion continues the decline of recent years. And nothing is replacing it. The reasons, of course, are diverse. Not the least important are the intricate policies devised by the Soviet government for "combating religion." Another strong influence is the comparatively "good times" achieved in part during the past decade. Organized religion has never really overcome the pathetic state that it allowed itself to fall into prior to the Revolution, and for this reason many conditions will have to change drastically before the public practice of a meaningful religion flourishes in Russia. Not only will religion have to regain public respect, but it will have to adapt itself to a brand new culture.

Robert Crane, an independent consultant on Sino-Soviet political and military affairs, probes Soviet military strategy. In his treatment of Soviet military power and thought patterns, Mr. Crane offers a hardheaded approach to understanding the makeup of a steadily improving armament posture. Both on the subliminal and conscious levels, he points out, new Soviet conditioning processes and international environmental factors are being set in motion to convey and support Soviet political global goals. The role of both long- and short-range intelligence estimates is crucial here. Unquestionably this chapter offers many valuable insights into the strategic tussle that occupies the serious thought of all world leaders.

Michel Garder, French expert on Soviet affairs, closes this volume with a provocative chapter on the dialectic between Soviet domestic and international politics. Here he dwells especially on the changing religious character of communism. The Soviet system, in his view, entails a theocratic system that is now undergoing the process of laicization, and the seeds of de-Stalinization are now leaving their marks on the structure of everyday life. Barring some major catastrophe, it is Colonel Garder's opinion that the Soviets in power cannot and will not be able to turn back the forces at work for greater liberalization and a more human society.

All the specialists collaborating in this study share the view that a new Russia is emerging in the late nineteen-sixties. Marxism as a monolithic ideology has clearly seen its better days. And the use of such tactics as the secret police, terror and mass intimidation to persuade the people to align themselves with the faction in power is no longer in the forefront. Though many myths still live on, many other ghosts and rituals continue to crumble each day. Only a prophet can account for the accidents and irrational aspects of history ahead, but it is impossible not to foresee even more tremendous changes in store for Russia and the rest of the world as historical processes accelerate at an increasingly swifter pace.

Denis Dirscherl, S. J.

# CONTENTS

# 1

## Issues and Leadership in Soviet Politics

RICHARD MILLS

FOR MANY decades foreign observers hardly knew what to make of Soviet politics. The bitter power struggles among the contenders for the leadership of the Party with fatal consequences for some of the participants, the massive purges of the nineteen-thirties which ultimately became a nationwide reign of terror, the near deification of Stalin, the monopolistic rule of a single political party turning into a personal dictatorship—it was on the basis of these chaotic raw materials that one had to make an attempt at interpreting Soviet politics. The chaos was, nevertheless, accompanied by a dictatorial stability, substantial economic growth and an increase in the nation's military might—achievements paid for by considerable deprivations of every description borne by the population.

It was only toward the end of Stalin's lifetime that the first systematic attempts were made in the West to describe and analyze the method of rule developed by the dictator. So the analysts were soon faced with the necessity of following a series of events which would provide, they hoped, some clues as to just how much of the Stalinist heritage would carry over into the new era.

Almost at once the principle of collective leadership was proclaimed by Stalin's heirs. Apparently, there was to be no more

Richard Mills is Assistant Professor of Political Science at Fordham University in New York.

arbitrary havoc wreaked by the whims of one man. The terror
apparatus was put out of the land-office business in which it had
been engaged, and the prison camps were gradually emptied. Also,
a modest improvement in the standard of living was effected. On
the other hand, the party showed no sign of being willing to tolerate any political competition, and soon the members of the collective leadership found themselves in an unfortunate and familiar
situation, a power struggle. It very much seemed that history was
repeating itself. Yet we know that Khrushchev, the man considered
by some as likely to become a new Stalin, was unceremoniously
turned out of office when a later power struggle took an unex-
pected turn in 1964.

The question which quite naturally arises in an observer's mind
is: why these apparently eternal power struggles? There is a relatively simple answer behind which lurk some complex reasons. The
simple answer is that, until April of 1966, the party had no formal
method of choosing its leader.

The reasons are to be found by considering some aspects of
party history. The original leader of the Party was Lenin, and
indeed he was in his day recognized without dispute by nearly
everyone in the Party. He had, after all, founded the Party, and he
possesed an abundance of leadership qualities and one of those
powerful personalities which tended to dominate those around him.
At the same time, he held no party post which set him apart from
anybody else: as member of the Politburo and the Central Committee he was first among equals, although a very outstanding first, to
be sure. Lenin's death inevitably left a vacuum which Stalin eventually filled by manipulating both political issues and politicians.

Stalin was aided in those endeavors by the fact that he happened
to hold a unique post which did set him apart from all other
contenders for power: he was General Secretary of the Party. And
after Lenin's death he proceeded to *make* it into what it has remained since, the position which carries with it the leadership of
the Party. Stalin in this way established a tradition, but it was one
beset with certain difficulties which did not become important until
after his death.

With Stalin gone it was necessary once again to fill a vacuum.

The problem lay in how to do it. Quite understandably, none of the leaders was anxious to have any one of his associates fill the vacuum *too* completely. Why run the risk of creating a new Stalin? Also troublesome was the absence of an established mechanism for choosing a General Secretary. True, with respect to voting procedures for filling a number of its higher offices the Party was to some extent governed by its rules, or, in other words, the Party's constitution. But while the rules in effect at Stalin's death provided for the election of the Party's top decision-making bodies, they did not mention the General Secretary, let alone say anything about the method of choosing him. As it was, it would have been superfluous to have said anything on the matter since even the elections just noted were in fact a meaningless exercise involving nothing more than the approval of an already selected list of names.

The rules did provide for the convocation of a Party Congress every four years. At this national party convention attended by some 2,000 delegates a Central Committee composed of about 300 members is elected. It in turn elects two smaller decision-making bodies, the Politburo and the Secretariat, each having about a dozen members. That was as far as the rules went, but for reasons which have to be inferred, the collective leadership decided to have the new General Secretary, Khrushchev, "elected" by the Central Committee in September, 1953.[1] There is little doubt that this act merely ratified a decision which had been made earlier by the members of the Politburo.

There is far less certainty about the reasons prompting the Politburo to bring the Central Committee into the act. The Committee had practically fallen into disuse after Stalin's accession to power, playing an ever decreasing role and finally no role at all in choosing the members of the Politburo. It therefore came as something of a surprise to see the Committee called upon to ratify the already chosen General Secretary. Perhaps there was an attempt

[1] It has to be noted that Khrushchev's official title was changed to First Secretary, and the Politburo's name was changed to read Presidium. Since the older terms have been revived in the meantime, they shall be used throughout the discussion in these pages in order to avoid confusion.

here to revert to precedent. After all, only once before had a General Secretary been chosen, back in April, 1922. The then much smaller Central Committee elected Stalin to fill that newly created post, which lacked completely the significance it was later to assume through the tireless efforts of Stalin in his own behalf.

The power struggle which began after Stalin's death came to a head in June, 1957, when Khrushchev's position was challenged seriously by the so-called Anti-Party Group, an alliance of convenience among certain of the major political figures who were, generally speaking, proponents of a return to more authoritarian forms of rule. This episode was accompanied by a very revealing disagreement among the leaders as to just who had the right to decide the fate of the top leader. While the Anti-Party Group maintained that the Politburo was really empowered to pass on the question, Khrushchev insisted that since he had been elected to the post by the Central Committee, only the Committee could remove him. Interestingly enough, both sides were in effect appealing to different precedents in party history: Khrushchev to his 1953 "election," his opponents to the practices characteristic of the heyday of Stalinism when the Central Committee had no part to play in such matters. Because neither side was powerful enough to impose its view, and because the rules were silent on the leadership question, the outcome hinged upon practical politics of an extremely delicate and complex nature, which resulted in the convocation of the Central Committee and Khrushchev's victory.

That outcome enhanced Khrushchev's personal power immeasurably. And it all predictably went to his head. Although there was still some opposition to him in the top echelons of the Party, his position was nevertheless secure enough for a time to allow him the luxury of making a number of arbitrary decisions which served only to create an opposition with strength sufficient to unseat him in October, 1964. We unfortunately do not yet know as much about this event as we do of the 1957 confrontation. But the Central Committee once again played a pivotal role in determining the fate of the General Secretary, on this occasion finding it not worthwhile to support him. So, for the first time in Soviet history the Party's leader was removed from office by means of a vote. Brezhnev was elected in his place.

This was not, however, the first time that the leader had been elected by a vote. We have only to recall that there had been two votes taken by the Central Committee in earlier years. If the "election" in September, 1953, did not really make Khrushchev leader (there was still too much opposition to him in the Party's upper ranks), the defeat of the Anti-Party Group in June, 1957, certainly did—for a while. Here were two precedents, two responses to the realities of party politics in the Soviet Union which had no basis in the Party's rules. But now they do, since the rules were amended in April, 1966, to include the provision that the General Secretary is to be elected by the Central Committee.

Here is a matter requiring further consideration. The amendment does not mention the length of time the General Secretary is to serve in office. But as we already know, the rules have for quite some time provided for the election of the Party's highest decision-making bodies every four years. Although not stipulated in the rules, in practice since the death of Stalin the General Secretary was effortlessly reelected on those occasions, which understandably led Western observers to conclude that such elections were engineered and therefore meaningless. These conclusions represent only part of the story, for there have been two elections involving the General Secretary which were meaningful—the one in 1957 which saved Khrushchev, and the one in 1964 which retired him.

Both elections were significant because they indicated that the General Secretary's power had been challenged effectively. It is important to keep in mind that the challenge did not come from the Central Committee, but from the Politburo, from the inner circle of leadership. What came from the Committee once it had gathered in emergency session was a decision which either vindicated or rejected the General Secretary. Viewed against the background of these events it appears that the General Secretary's tenure continues until he loses the confidence of both the Politburo and the Central Committee.

Ultimately, Khrushchev was removed in 1964 because he could no longer control the Central Committee in the face of the apparently unanimous opposition to him within the Politburo, whereas in 1957 at least a minority had supported him within the Politburo. In short, Khrushchev was isolated in 1964 as he had never been before, and that isolation was partly the result of the reaction on the part of other Soviet political leaders to his style of decision-making, partly a consequence of the decisions themselves.

The major charges lodged against Khrushchev immediately after his removal were that the decisions made by him had been hasty, ill-advised and "subjective." The last complaint is perhaps the most important, involving as it does a rather touchy issue in Soviet politics. "Subjective" is one of those neat semantic evasions which had to be used to avoid the embarrassment of saying that Khrushchev's decisions had been taking on an increasingly arbitrary character. Unfortunately, the term arbitrary had been much used by Khrushchev since 1956 to describe the character of Stalin's rule. To have used that word in 1964 would have carried with it the unflattering implication that perhaps not that much had changed in party politics at the top. There were, indeed, signs in the last years of Khrushchev's rule that something naggingly reminiscent of the "Cult of the Personality" was reappearing. Therefore, subjectivism in decision-making figured rather prominently as a factor in Khrushchev's removal.

Credit must be given where credit is due. The members of the Politburo and the Central Committee saw history beginning to repeat itself, and they took action, a kind of action which would soon have been impossible had the arbitrariness been allowed to follow its normal course of development. Already an unhealthy pattern of events had emerged in the early nineteen-sixties: some arbitrary decisions had resulted in failure, only to be followed by boastful claims of success which were amplified by a claque headed by none other than Khrushchev's son-in-law, Alexi Adzhubei, at the time editor of the major daily newspaper *Izvestia*. One could hardly fail to recognize here the old Stalinist ploy of transforming real failures into imaginary victories by means of propagandistic incantations. Such antics had never quite disappeared from the post-Stalin scene in the Soviet Union, but toward the end of Khrushchev's rule they again assumed a menacingly large role. It was a question of degree, and the point was fast approaching where the nation would once more be living in the rarefied atmosphere of fantasy and delusion with all their attendant furies. This melancholy chain of events was broken by Khrushchev's ouster.

The conclusion which emerges from what has been said is that it has apparently become harder to control the Central Committee. Perhaps that body has in fact recovered some of the vitality which it lost in the nineteen-twenties. Only time will really tell. Clearly, the Central Committee's significance in Soviet politics has increased since 1957. A word might also be said about the growth in the Committee's sophistication, supporting as it did in both 1957 and 1964 the side in the leadership struggle which showed the most promise of steering the country away from Stalinist paths. In 1957 it happened to have been Khrushchev; in 1964, after he had been spoiled by having amassed too much power, it was his opponents. Times had changed, and so had people.

The Party, however, still has some distance to go before it can ensure the smooth replacement of its leader. Part of the problem has been tackled by establishing clearly in the rules who has the right to choose the Party's head. Over and above the possibility that the new rule may either be changed or not observed in the future, there is the crucial business of how alternative leaders and policies can get a hearing. There is also the question of the extent to which any opposition can exist within the Party.

To say that the very word "opposition" has long been an obscenity in the Party's political vocabulary would do little violence to the truth. The Party has for decades been obsessed with the idea of creating and maintaining a monolithic unity with its ranks. Consequently, the official textbooks dealing with the Party's history devote considerable space to a seemingly endless series of struggles against oppositions of all descriptions which have cropped up within the Party. The object lesson to be derived from party history is crystal clear: do not oppose the policies of the Party. If everybody heeded that admonition there would be almost no politics in the Party. Moreover, the members of the higher leadership cannot observe that rule inasmuch as it is up to them to decide not only what the Party's policy is to be, but also what changes in policy seem advisable. It is the unavoidable need to make these kinds of decisions which gives rise to politics and, eventually, opposition.

After Stalin's death the extent of disagreement among the higher leaders increased. But due to the excessive concern with maintaining a facade of unity, everybody involved was reluctant to have their disagreements aired in public. Only by a very careful reading of these men's speeches could analysts of Soviet politics sort out the opposing sides by noting what the various leaders emphasized, omitted or understated when discussing policy issues. There existed a mutual understanding among the leaders with respect to how far it was possible to go publicly in airing differences of opinion. What went on at the private meetings of the Politburo or the secret sessions of the Central Committee was quite another matter. From the little that is known about these meetings it appears that the arguments were often heated. But once a decision was taken all were expected to adhere to it, and in their public statements they more or less did. For that reason sudden shifts in policy, and the casualties among the major leaders which often enough accompanied them, tended to catch outside observers by surprise. That was especially true of the biggest surprise of recent years, Khrushchev's removal. To be sure, there had from time to time been rumors, generally originating in Vienna, that his removal was imminent, and there were certain specialists in Soviet affairs in the West who noted that there was considerably more opposition to Khrushchev than was commonly assumed. However, nobody was rash enough to venture a prediction as to how and when he would be overthrown.

It has been noted that one of the primary factors behind Khrushchev's ouster was the dissatisfaction with his style of leadership. Many of the other issues involved may be grouped under the heading of disagreements over economic policy. In particular, the new leadership, once in power, showed that it was more willing than Khrushchev had been to increase budgetary spending for the purposes of developing agriculture and producing more consumer goods. There had been a good deal of talk about these matters in the Soviet Union during Khrushchev's last years in office. His general position then could be described as trying to get blood out of a stone, or, putting it even more bluntly, attempting to get something for nothing. The whole idea worked as badly in socialist Russia as it does under more capitalist conditions.

Since Khrushchev found it convenient to explain away the resultant failures of his policy as consequences of poor arrangements in government and party organization, he seized upon reorganization as the most likely remedy for the country's economic ills. The nation therefore embarked upon what eventually turned into a veritable orgy of reorganizations. As each new reorganization failed to produce the promised results the cumulative confusion and inefficiency reached monumental proportions. The numerous party members whose main responsibility consisted in attempting to make all these reorganizations work were thereby put in a highly tenuous position, because they were being asked to do the impossible. Small wonder that Khrushchev was unable to garner much support when the time came to apportion the blame at the October, 1964, Central Committee session.

Perhaps the greatest opposition to Khrushchev was engendered by his decision, which came like a bolt out of the blue, to effect a drastic reorganization of the Party into two branches: one for industry, the other for agriculture. Since, in effect, the Party was split in two, there was a very real danger that the interests represented by both branches would eventually find themselves in a face-to-face confrontation over issues such as the relative share of money which the urban and rural areas of the country ought to get from the national budget. Obviously, party unity was threatened, and there is some evidence that this reorganization was the straw which broke the camel's back, being viewed as an encroachment upon the Party's fundamental and traditional principle of organization. It was seen that what Khrushchev was doing was putting himself *above* the Party. Back in 1956 Khrushchev had some rather harsh words to say about Stalin for having done the same thing in the nineteen-thirties. Apparently, this slipped Khrushchev's mind—but there were others who remembered.

With Khrushchev gone Soviet politics entered into a period of almost boring calm by comparison with what had taken place just before. Two months after the new leadership had assumed power the Party was reunited, undoing with little apparent pain and strain Khrushchev's earlier handiwork. Thereafter the leadership's attention was pretty much devoted to working out and overseeing the implementation of policies calculated to improve the performance of agriculture and industry. In the process, the Brezhnev-Kosygin team developed an image of businesslike pragmatism in searching for solutions to the nation's most pressing economic problems. By April, 1966, the main guidelines of a new Five-Year Plan were worked out and approved at the Twenty-third Party Congress.

It was at this Congress that the titles General Secretary and Politburo were revived. The reasons for these actions are not entirely clear. At the time some students of Soviet politics saw ominous portents in this return to the terminology of the Stalin era. So far, little has happened to justify those fears.

The Twenty-third Congress was a kind of capstone for the new leadership, the final decision-making step in the process of eliminating Khrushchev's errors and establishing a new direction in domestic policy. Afterward there was a notable switch of attention to foreign affairs, a field which had been somewhat neglected during the leadership's preoccupation with internal problems.

Seemingly, the party leaders have returned to a system of rule by consensus among themselves. So far it has worked surprisingly well. The leaders have taken their time in working out decisions, apparently resolving disagreements rather than imposing hastily made decisions. How long this policy will last is anybody's guess. In part, success in maintaining the consensus is attributable to the fact that certain difficult issues have been put off for quite some time. There are, for instance, the problems of the Soviet constitution and the charter governing the operation of the collective farms. Both documents were adopted in the nineteen-thirties, and are now out of date in many respects. Two commissions were long ago appointed to revise them. The job is not an easy one, because it entails making a number of major decisions on such questions as the extent to which autonomy is to be granted to the local authorities, the precise relationship of the Party to the government and a host of equally delicate matters. In other words, the commissions must confront a variety of issues involving power relationships and ideological problems, two areas which in the past have been extremely fertile in provoking serious disagreements.

These considerations lead us directly into the sphere of what may be termed "unproblems" in Soviet politics. Issues such as the status of the many nationalities which make up the population, the question of intellectual and artistic freedom, the autonomy of what might be termed interest groups, and religious freedom are officially considered not to exist. Nevertheless, time and again problems arise in all these areas, even though the Party is highly intolerant of them. As the economic situation improves, it appears likely that civil rights will increasingly command the attention of the party leaders. Because the population is becoming better educated and more sophisticated the Party can be expected to experience considerable difficulty in exercising the kind of control it managed to impose in the past.

Much of what has been said above points toward a growing maturity in Soviet politics. Hopeful though the sign may be, that maturity is still in its early stages and is susceptible to a multitude of hazards. Still, in many respects, the present situation in the Soviet Union reminds one of Russia in the late nineteenth century, when the country was beginning to outgrow its autocratic form of government. The autocracy's resistance to the pressures coming from the more articulate segments of the population only served to create an impasse which ultimately led to the demise of the government. If this parallel has any validity at all, then some really critical decisions await the party leadership in the not too distant future.

There may be more hope in this regard than might at first be imagined. Since the death of Stalin the Party has gradually seen fit to narrow the scope of its control; some areas of Soviet life have been taken out of the realm of politics. It used to be that there was an orthodox stand to be taken by all citizens on everything from abstract philosophical propositions to fashions in clothing. The Party slowly learned—and it was a learning process—how to become more discriminating in choosing the areas where that kind of control was really critical. It also managed to place greater faith in the citizenry at large. Toward the end of the nineteen-fifties some parts of the country were opened to travel by foreigners. The resultant exposure of the population to influences which the Party had for so long tried to combat soon made it senseless to jam foreign radio broadcasts beamed to the Soviet Union, and that costly operation was shut down. The people are consequently better informed.

The Party also became more responsive to the demands of the population for more housing and consumer goods. In the process, some of the old ideological dogmatism in economic theory was discarded with little attempt at justification—that problem was passed over in silence. It was recognized implicitly that experimentation and criticism had an important role to play in economic decision-making.

The important question is, will these new flexible attitudes be transferred to politics? So far, there is little real evidence pointing in that direction. Only once has the suggestion been made in public —there is no way of telling what kind of wild ideas crop up in private discussion—that it might be a good idea to allow a number of people to run in each voting district for election to the Supreme Soviet, the Russian parliament. So extraordinary is this proposal that it has to be put into the "man bites dog" category. It will be very interesting to see just how much support this almost subversive idea eventually generates.

There have also been some suggestions that the authority of the local governments be strengthened, a less novel departure from Soviet tradition than the idea of multiple candidacy. The implication is that less spoon-feeding on the part of the national government is needed now that there are more people at the local level who are capable of managing their own affairs.

The party leadership has not yet responded to these initiatives. In one way or another it will do so when the new draft constitution is formally proposed and discussed. The struggle for progress thus will continue, with all its ups and downs.

Whatever the results of the discussions connected with the constitution, in rapidly changing societies solutions to problems, and even "unproblems," as often as not turn out to be temporary. Constant readjustments are called for by new developments in both thought and action. The Soviet Union is still in a very delicate stage of transition from dictatorship to a more representative form of government. That process can be arrested or reversed, but apparently only with increasing difficulty and at the considerable risk of undermining the political stability of the country, which would create an illusory kind of strength such as has been characteristic of highly authoritarian regimes just before they collapsed.

# 2

# New and Not So New in the Soviet Economy*

ARTHUR W. WRIGHT

THE RECENT golden anniversary of the Great October Revolution of 1917 finds the Soviet economy at the center of attention of Russian leaders and foreign observers alike, and likely to remain there for some time to come. The concern for economic affairs has not sprung up overnight. There were strong economic overtones to the removal in October, 1964, of Nikita S. Khrushchev from his top posts in both the Communist party and the government. It was no accident that he was replaced as government premier by Alexei N. Kosygin, an industrial management and planning expert. Moreover, economic problems and proposed solutions have preoccupied most recent plenary sessions of the party Central Committee and the important Twenty-third Party Congress held in the spring of 1966.[1]

---

\* Much of the material in this chapter appeared in the author's "The Soviet Economy" in *Current History*, October 1966. © Current History Inc., 1966.

[1] Recent plenary sessions of the Communist Party of the Soviet Union (CPSU) and their agendas, in chronological order:

    October 14, 1964—removal of Khrushchev
    November 16, 1964—major change in the party economic-administrative apparatus
    March 24-26, 1965—agricultural policy proposals; reports on international party meetings
    September 27-29, 1965—planning and management changes

Arthur W. Wright is Assistant Professor of Economics at Oberlin College, Oberlin, Ohio.

Behind all the attention to economic matters lie some basic questions of Soviet economic policy and practice. Chief among them is a lagging rate of economic growth. Directly related problems include a weak agricultural sector, a creaking industrial planning system, and pressure for larger defense outlays and more consumer goods—for more guns *and* more butter. The ferment attending these problems indicates novelty and change. Yet the "novelty" in the Soviet economy is easily exaggerated: all of the problems, and some of the remedies which have been mooted, trace their roots back at least a decade. A bit of background, therefore, will help to identify the pressures for change and interpret the responses of Soviet policy makers to those pressures.

## I. *Soviet Development in Perspective*

One feature of the Soviet economy which definitely is not new is rapid change. The Soviet period of Russian history is after all a mere half century. Of that period, three years were taken up by a bitter civil war—hard on the heels of the devastation of World War I—and a decade more by preparing for, waging and recovering from World War II. In the remaining time, the Russian economy has been transformed from a largely rural, peasant-smallhold condition with only a small and decrepit industrial sector, into the world's second largest modern industrial economy. Whether or not one likes the process used to effect the transformation, it was certainly rapid.

The new Bolshevik government in late 1917 inherited a budding but wartorn industrial base from its tsarist and "provisional" pred-

---

February 19, 1966—draft directives of the new five-year plan (1966-1970)

May 25-27, 1966—major agricultural land reclamation proposals

August 1, 1966—questions to arise at the upcoming first session of the seventh Supreme Soviet (government legislative body) of the Soviet Union on August 2-3, 1966

December 12-13, 1966—international Communist movement; draft annual economic plan for 1967; state budget for 1967.

The Twenty-third Party Congress, March 29-April 9, 1966, was devoted to Brezhnev's "state of the union" report, Kosygin's report on the new five-year plan, and assorted party business.

ecessors. The first dozen or so years of its life were devoted, first, to securing the revolution, and then to recovering from war. During the years 1918 to 1920, a period known as "War Communism," peace was made with the external enemy in the World War, and war declared on the internal enemy in a civil war. Next came the "New Economic Policy" (NEP) of 1921-1928, a time of breath-catching, stock-taking and heated debate about the future. By the end of the nineteen-twenties Soviet leaders were ready to embark on the first of a sequence of five-year plans [2] that were to build up the industrial sector at an unprecedented pace. Their policy rested on two major programs: (1) investment in capacity that would create more capacity (basic metals, machinery and Lenin's favorite, electrification), and (2) collectivization of peasant agriculture. There is not space here to go into the fascinating course of strategy debates and tactical shifts, or the staggering administrative problems and human consequences involved in driving the peasants from their smallholds into the collectives.[3] Suffice it to say that Soviet industrial capacity has grown mightily, and that the collectivization fulfilled the main task set for it: provisioning the burgeoning heavy industrial sector with vital raw materials, food and

[2] The first actual state plan was "Plan for the Electrification of Russia" (Plan GOELRO), announced in 1920-21, which had a ten to fifteen year horizon, and was correspondingly vague on specific details. The five-year plans *per se* are as follows, chronologically:

First Five-Year Plan (FYP), 1928/9-1932/3 (refers to the old Russian harvest calendar; in 1930, the plan periods were converted to standard calendar years)
Second FYP, 1933-1937
Third FYP, 1938-1942 (interrupted by the "Great Patriotic War")
Fourth FYP, 1946-1950
Fifth FYP, 1951-1955
Sixth FYP, 1956-1960 (abandoned in 1957)
The Seven-Year Plan, 1959-1965
Eighth FYP, 1966-1970.

[3] The debates are discussed in Alexander Erlich, *The Soviet Industrialization Debates* (Cambridge: Harvard University Press, 1960); and Nicolas Spulber, *Soviet Strategy for Economic Growth* (Bloomington: Indiana University Press, 1964). On the collectivization, see Lionel Kochan, *The Making of Modern Russia* (Baltimore: Penguin Books, 1963), pp. 283-290; and Maurice Dobb, *Soviet Economic Development since 1917* (New York: International Publishers, 1966), chapter 9.

labor, in larger quantities and at lower cost—to the State if not to the peasants—than would have been possible under even an improved version of the old system. In spite of substantial shortcomings, especially recently, the collective farm [4] is still an important feature of Soviet agriculture.

The rapid and extensive mobilization of resources required for the "industrialization drive" was achieved by the development of the Soviet industrial planning system. The basic purpose of Soviet planning was, and remains, the avoidance of the "anarchy" of capitalist markets by maintaining effective central control over resource allocation. Such control can in principle be achieved either through absolute centralization of every decision; or through centralization of only the basic outlines of policy, implementing them with incentives which channel lower level decisions, made in the individual's self-interest, into plan fulfillment.

The first alternative was never a real one for the Russians: their economy was just too big, economically and geographically, to cover every detail of economic life from Moscow. But neither did they opt entirely for the second alternative, with its suggestion of private instead of social consciousness. What became known as Soviet planning was a mixture of (a) centralized policy-making with some direct central interference in implementation; (b) some deliberate decentralizing levers to encourage managers and workers in industrial enterprises to fulfill their plans; and (c) some *de facto* decentralization of decisions, which afforded flexibility but also diluted the sought after effectiveness of central control over the final outcome.

For all its faults—and many indeed have been pointed out over the years—the Soviet planning system did mobilize resources for a dramatic record of economic growth. Whether another system could or would have produced better results—with all other factors constant—must remain an academic question. The question of possible changes is not so academic, however, as is amply illustrated by the current debates over planning reforms.

[4] The Soviet collective farm (or *kolkhoz*) is a producer cooperative, with only household goods and a small garden plot held privately. The other type of agricultural unit, the state farm (or *sovkhoz*) hires wageworkers to till the land, and functions as an industrial enterprise, with a manager.

## II. *The Lagging Rate of Economic Growth*

There can be little doubt that the principal impetus for reform is the decline since about 1958 in Soviet rates of growth of total output and, what is worse, industrial output. Tables 1 and 2 give estimates of recent Soviet growth rates for gross national product (GNP) and "national income," and for industrial output. Figures are given for the United States to emphasize the implications of the Soviet deceleration—and the recent American acceleration—for the economic race which the Soviet leaders are committed to winning. The narrower the gap between the growth rates, the longer the time required for the Soviet Union to "overtake and surpass" the United States.[5] It should be emphasized that the decline has occurred in *rates* of growth, not absolute magnitudes; and Soviet growth rates still exceed those of the United States but to a much smaller degree.

What can be said of the causes of the decline? In principle, all changes in the rate of growth are ascribable to changes in the *quantities* of inputs—labor, capital and natural resources of various types—and to changes in their *qualities,* or *productivities.* Tentatively, American observers [6] now think that labor input (employment) has risen substantially in the last decade, but the rate of increase in the Soviet capital stock (investment) has tapered off. On the qualitative side, both labor and capital productivity have

[5] For example, suppose the American GNP were twice the Soviet level (approximately the relative positions of the two countries at present). If the average annual growth rates of GNP for the U.S.A. and the Soviet Union were 2.9% and 7.1% respectively (as in 1950-58—see Table 1), the Russians would overtake the Americans in less than seventeen years. But if the rates were instead 4.4% and 5.3% (as in 1958-64), the overtaking time would exceed seventy-seven years!

[6] The most recent and complete estimates can be found in a compendium published by the Joint Economic Committee of the United States Congress, entitled *New Directions in the Soviet Economy* (five volumes), Washington, 1966; especially the papers by Stanley H. Cohn (pp. 99-132) and James H. Noren (pp. 271-326). This compendium is the latest in a useful series on the Soviet economy put out by the Joint Economic Committee since 1960. In chronological order: *Comparisons of the United States and Soviet Economies* (three volumes, 1960); *Dimensions of Soviet Economic Power* (one volume with hearings, 1962); *Annual Economic Indicators for U.S.S.R.* (one volume, 1964); *Current Economic Indicators for the U.S.S.R.* (one volume, 1965).

**Table 1. Soviet and American Growth Rates of Gross National Product and "National Income"**

(average annual percentage increases)

a. Gross National Product (American definition) *

|  | Total | | Per Capita | |
|---|---|---|---|---|
|  | U.S.S.R. | U.S.A. | U.S.S.R. | U.S.A. |
| 1950-1958 | 7.1 | 2.9 | 5.2 | 1.2 |
| 1958-1964 | 5.3 | 4.4 | 3.5 | 2.7 |

b. "National Income" (Soviet definition) *

|  | Total | | Per Capita | |
|---|---|---|---|---|
|  | U.S.S.R. | U.S.A. | U.S.S.R. | U.S.A. |
| 1950-1958 | 10.9 | 2.5 | 9.0 | 1.0 |
| 1958-1964 ** | 6.8 | 4.3 | 5.1 | 2.5 |

Sources: (a) S. Cohn, in U.S. Congress (89th-2), Joint Economic Committee, **New Directions in the Soviet Economy,** Washington, 1966, Part II-A, p. 105.

(b) **Narodnoe khoziaistvo SSSR v 1964 godu: statisticheskii yezhegodnik** (National Economy of the USSR in 1964: Statistical Annual), Moscow, 1965, p. 88.

* The gross national product (American definition) represents the total value of final goods and services produced in an economy during a given period (usually a year); in other words, consumption, investment (including replacement) and government services. Soviet "national income" differs from American national income concepts chiefly in the exclusion of "unproductive" sectors' outputs: e.g., teachers' salaries, government administration, health services, housing. etc. Karl Marx (following Adam Smith) distinguished between **productive** activities (consumer and capital goods plus transportation) and **unproductive** activities (services plus nonproductive construction). Both sorts of activities, of course, entail the use of scarce resources, which is why American national income accountants include "unproductive" outputs in their calculations. Because services and housing are relatively more important in the American than the Soviet economy, the Soviet concept of "national income" tends to show a greater discrepancy between Soviet and American growth rates than the gross national product figures.

** According to the Soviet statistical annual for 1965, p. 86, the 1958-1965 figures are (left to right) 6.9, 4.5, 5.3 and 2.8.

### Table 2.  Soviet Industrial Growth Rates

(average annual percentage increases)

a. Industrial Production, Value-Added Basis
   (American definition) *

|  |  |
|---|---|
| 1950-1958 | 10.5 |
| 1958-1965 | 7.9 |

Alternative time-periods:

|  |  |
|---|---|
| 1950-1955 | 11.2 |
| 1955-1958 | 9.5 |
| 1958-1961 | 8.6 |
| 1961-1965 | 7.3 |

b. Industrial Production, Gross Output Basis
   (Soviet definition) *

|  |  | (U.S.A.) |
|---|---|---|
| 1950-1958 | 12.1 | 2.8 |
| 1958-1965 | 9.1 | 6.3 |

Alternative time-periods:

|  |  |
|---|---|
| 1950-1955 | 13.1 |
| 1955-1958 | 10.3 |
| 1958-1961 | 10.0 |
| 1961-1965 | 8.5 |

Sources: (a) J. Noren, in **New Directions, op. cit.** (Table 1),
Part II-A, pp. 280-281.

(b) **Narodnoe khoziaistvo SSSR v 1965 godu: statisticheskii yezhegodnik** (National Economy of the
USSR in 1965: Statistical Annual), Moscow,
1966, pp. 92, 122.

* Soviet "gross industrial output" counts the value of an industrial
product each time it leaves a plant in the production process from raw
materials to finished goods. For example, a loaf of bread would be
"double counted" at the grain elevator, the mill, the bakery and the pack-
aging plant, as well as on the shelf. By contrast, in the American value-
added approach only the **additional** resources used up at each stage of
production are counted in industrial output. In other words, the loaf of
bread would be counted only on the shelf, or equivalently, its total value
would equal the sum of "value-added" at each stage of production.

fallen. The former may be due largely to having to add many relatively unproductive workers, principally women, young adults and migrants from farming, because of the manpower losses of World War II and the accompanying low birthrates after the war. The decline in capital productivity arises from several sources, including "diminishing returns" to investment, the lower productivity labor force, and perhaps most of all, difficulties in planning, a topic about which more will be said later. A declining growth rate is readily seen, then, as the net effect of one positive but three negative influences.

The evidence just cited is suggestive but not as yet hard and fast. Fortunately, though, one may turn to four specific areas—agriculture, industrial planning, consumption levels and defense-and space-spending—for information which indirectly sheds further light on the slipping growth rates.

## III. *Agriculture*

In the apt phrase of Khrushchev's successor as First Party Secretary, Leonid I. Brezhnev, Soviet agriculture has been "marking time" in recent years. Instead of the dramatic seventy percent increase envisioned for the seven-year plan of 1959 to 1965, total agricultural output experienced only a slightly rising trend of ten percent—aggravated by sharp year-to-year fluctuations. In particular, the failure of grain output to match expectations has caused shortages of bread, fodder and meat.

The overall Soviet economic growth rate has been influenced in two ways by the lag in agricultural output. First, poor performance in a major sector of the economy, contributing some twenty-five percent of national income, has dragged down the average rate for the whole economy. Second, lagging supplies of raw materials for industry, and the necessity to expend precious foreign exchange— itself cut by curtailed food exports—on imported food, have held back the growth of the crucial industrial sector.

An idea of the causes of such poor performance can be gained from a look at Soviet agricultural policies since Stalin.[7] As indi-

[7] See Sidney Ploss's interesting study, *Conflict and Decision-Making in Soviet Russia: A Case Study of Agricultural Policy, 1953-63* (Princeton: Princeton University Press, 1965).

cated previously, agriculture played a vital role in the early stages of industrialization. By the close of the fourth five-year plan in 1950, however, Soviet agriculture was showing signs of exhaustion. The reason lay in inadequate reimbursement over the previous two decades with machinery, fertilizer and other vital agricultural inputs for all the food, raw materials and labor pumped from agriculture to sustain industrial growth. Moreover, farmers' incentives in the form of real incomes and available consumer goods were inadequate to stimulate agricultural output and marketings. It was time for a "new deal" for Russian agriculture.

Such a new deal was not then in the cards, however. At the death of Stalin in March, 1953, his successors disagreed in their evaluations of the true extent of the crisis in agriculture. Georgi M. Malenkov, who, as a close Stalin aide, bore great responsibility for the neglect which underlay the crisis, attempted to cover it over by tapping emergency grain reserves for current consumption. Others, for example, Nikolai Bulganin, were too taken up with heavy industry to worry about agriculture. One man—Nikita S. Khrushchev —had tried in vain for several years to persuade Stalin of the deterioration of agriculture, and after Stalin's death he set about garnering support for an extensive agricultural program—to be staffed by his political supporters, of course. His failure on the whole to win such support then and throughout his tenure in office is a great irony of Soviet politics. For one of his successors' first moves (discussed further below) was to map out the long overdue new deal for agriculture, substantially along the lines advocated by Khrushchev for a decade and a half.

Khrushchev did manage, though, to sell his "virgin lands" program. The key to this scheme was additional land inputs on a massive scale—some thirty million hectares (seventy-four million acres) plowed up within three years in southern European Russia, Siberia, and northern Kazakhstan. The program's appeal lay in the substitution of the new lands for labor and capital inputs, which then did not have to be drawn away from industry. Also appealing was the organization of the new lands into "state" farms (see footnote 4 above), ideologically preferable to the peasant collectives, because they employ wageworkers.

The virgin lands campaign drew fire both at home and abroad.

**Table 3.   Soviet Grain Harvests and State Procurements**

(millions of metric tons; 1 metric ton = 2,204.6 lbs.)

| | Harvests * | | Procurements | |
| | Total | Virgin Lands | Total | Virgin Lands |
|---|---|---|---|---|
| | (1) | (2) | (3) | (4) |
| 1953 | 82.5 | 27.1 | 31.1 | 10.9 |
| 1954 | 85.6 | 37.6 | 34.6 | 17.8 |
| 1955 | 103.7 | 28.0 | 36.9 | 11.3 |
| 1956 | 125.0 | 63.6 | 54.1 | 36.8 |
| 1957 | 102.6 | 38.5 | 35.4 | 17.0 |
| 1958 | 134.7 | 58.8 | 56.6 | 32.8 |
| 1959 | 119.5 | 55.3 | 46.6 | 27.9 |
| 1960 | 125.5 | 59.1 | 46.7 | 29.1 |
| 1961 | 130.8 | 51.3 | 52.1 | 23.8 |
| 1962 | 140.2 | 56.4 | 56.6 | 27.1 |
| 1963 | 107.5 | 37.9 | 44.8 | 16.3 |
| 1964 | 152.1 | n.a. | 68.3 | 37.5 |
| 1965 | 121.1 | n.a. | 36.3 | n.a. |
| 1966 | 170.8 | n.a. | n.a. | n.a. |

n.a. = not available.

Sources: column (1) 1953-1964: **Narodnoe khoziaistvo SSSR v 1964 g.: statisticheskii yezhegodnik** (National Economy of the USSR in 1964: Statistical Annual), Moscow, 1965, p. 295.

column (1) 1965-1966: **Ekonomika sel'skogo khoziaistva** (Economics of Agriculture), 1967, No. 2, p. 4.

column (3) 1953-1964: **Narodnoe khoziaistvo . . . 1964 g., op. cit.**, p. 295; **Narodnoe khoziaistvo . . . 1965 g.**, p. 311.

columns (2) and (4): **Narodnoe khoziaistvo . . . , op. cit.**, various years, 1958-1964.

\* These figures are so-called "barn yields," not "biological" or on-the-stalk, and exclude "corn of milk-wax ripeness," i.e., green corn of relatively low food value. In recent years the Soviet statistical annuals have ceased reporting green corn, although in the late nineteen-fifties and early nineteen-sixties it was included in total grain harvests, sometimes without an adjusted figure exclusive of it.

If one views the program after the fact, the criticisms appear justified. Initial rapid increases in output gave way after the bumper crop of 1958 to a record that was at best mediocre, at worst disastrous (see Table 3). In addition, machinery and other resources had to be diverted from other agricultural regions, no doubt causing substandard performances there, and in many areas of the new lands, "dust bowl" conditions have arisen from poor soil management mixed with drought.

Yet, if one waives the advantages of hindsight, from the perspective of the early nineteen-fifties the virgin lands campaign seems less poorly chosen. The near crisis state of agriculture in 1953 demanded that something be done, on pain of facing bread riots or importing large quantities of food. In light of the near crisis and the political opposition to a full-scale assault on agricultural problems, the campaign was not a "hare-brained scheme" but an ingenious stopgap designed to rescue a desperate grain situation, as least temporarily, at what promised to be quite low cost.

Then what happened, it may be asked, to turn a sound idea in prospect into a hare-brained scheme in retrospect? The answer seems to be that temporary expedients become poor solutions if maintained more than temporarily. Besides the poor soil management already cited, a factor further tending to undermine the longer run success of the new lands policy was inadequate adaptation of existing techniques to the particular conditions encountered. For example, seed types and fertilizers suited to semi-arid climates were not made available on a wide scale. Lack of proper adaptation heightened the sensitivity of the crops to variations in the weather, with grave consequences in 1963 and 1965. But we should recall here that such adaptation would have entailed large-scale outlays, the avoidance of which was the attraction of the virgin lands scheme in the first place. And adaptation probably would not have been so crucial if the program had remained a stopgap as initially intended.

The problems of the virgin lands are in many respects caricatures of Soviet agricultural problems as a whole. With little exaggeration Soviet agricultural policy over the years can be summed up as an attempt to obtain production "on the cheap." This policy worked initially. It could also be salvaged for a few extra years by the virgin lands campaign. But ultimately it has had to be reconsidered in the face of stagnating agricultural output: low production levels, even on the cheap, can be expensive in terms of economic growth.

Secretary Brezhnev chose the March, 1965, plenum of the party Central Committee to outline the "new" approach to agriculture. The diagnosis was basically Khrushchev's—capital resources and farmer incentives—and the policy recommendations followed the diagnosis. The "material-technical base" of agriculture was to be enhanced by a 100 percent increase in capital investments financed from the government budget [8] during 1966-1970 as compared to 1961-1965 by larger numbers of specialists and technicians accompanying better repair facilities provided on easier financial terms and by expanded government programs of agricultural research and training. The crop areas opened up in the virgin lands will remain in production, but the program will be "consolidated and developed" with more non-land resources.

As for incentives, state procurement policy is to be drastically overhauled in favor of the farmers: "planned" (required) deliveries to the State will be reduced and stabilized for a six-year period, and will be bought by the State at higher base prices. The farms will also be able to sell above-plan output to the State at prices fifty per cent higher than the base procurement prices. Further, collective farms are to be treated more equally on taxes, electric power rates, and so on, as compared with the state farms. More generally, the collective farm has been reaffirmed as playing a vital role in "building the material-technical base of communism," in contrast to past pressures to convert the collectives into state farms.

The above proposals were reaffirmed in their entirety at the Twenty-third Party Congress in the spring of 1966. Party leaders also announced an ambitious plan, elaborated upon at the Central Committee plenum of May, 1966, to reclaim, lime or irrigate an additional forty-six million hectares (114 million acres, equal to over one-fifth of present total sown area) of substandard land. The

[8] Heretofore, the collective farms have been made to fulfill their investment plans largely from their own resources, the state farms to a lesser degree.

new five-year plan goal for agricultural output, announced by Premier Kosygin at the congress, is a modest twenty-five percent increase in the average annual output over the average 1961-1965 level (which includes the bad harvests of 1963 and 1965). This goal should be realizable if even a portion of the above proposals is effected.[9] The modest size of the goal suggests that, in the opinion of the Soviet leadership, one dose of resources in five short years will not restore a long ailing agricultural sector to full health. Hence we should probably look for additional heavy commitments to agriculture beyond 1970.

## IV. *Industrial Planning*

In contrast to agriculture, the current problems of the Soviet industrial planning system arise from success rather than failure. Simply put, the old system has outgrown itself: put together originally to support rapid industrialization—as outlined earlier—of late it has not proven adaptable to the intricate tasks of efficiently running the massive industrial base which it helped to create. In the words of the draft directives of the new five-year plan,

> . . . in the past few years a disparity has formed between the sharply rising scale of production [on the one hand] and the methods of planning and economic management and the system of material incentives that were in effect [on the other]. . . .[10]

The relative simplicity of goals during the first generation of Soviet economic development, "Produce more steel to build more steel mills," made crash programs aimed at bottleneck sectors an effective means of achieving rapid growth. The old style planning system, emphasizing physical output levels of key products, was able to handle these crash programs, particularly to direct supplies and labor to the critical areas in a hurry. Industrial success, however, brought with it the necessity to keep track of ever larger numbers and varieties of products: now "produce more steel" had

[9] Soviet protestations to the contrary notwithstanding, the bumper crop of 1966 almost certainly cannot be explained by the new programs, whose benefits can hardly have begun to be felt even if they are well underway. It was much more likely due to extremely good weather in all growing regions.

[10] *Pravda* and *Izvestia*, February 20, 1966; translated in *Current Digest of the Soviet Press*, Vol. XVIII, No. 7 (March 9, 1966), p. 4.

to be broken down into a myriad of specifications to suit a myriad of users. The number of potential—and actual—bottlenecks increased: single-minded *shturmovshchiny* (storming campaigns) could no longer be designed and executed fast enough to deal with them all. As a consequence, actual economic results began to diverge sharply from the planners' intentions.

The Soviet press has always been filled with criticisms of this or that aspect of the planning system. In the late nineteen-fifties, however, the locus of the criticisms began to shift from superficial, hortatory treatments of isolated cases—"We must improve the planning of . . ."—to more basic, analytical discussions questioning the fundamental premises of the system. This shift coincided with the reemergence of the Soviet economics profession from an intellectual limbo dating back to the start of the industrialization effort in the early nineteen-thirties. The combination produced a full-fledged debate on the purposes, principles and methods of planning, a debate which is still in progress.

Two principal schools of thought (paralleling the two planning alternatives suggested in Part I above) stand out in the discussions. One holds that the exploitation of advancing computer technology to gather, process and analyze mountains of data would provide more effective centralized planning control, and avoid the undesirable *de facto* kind of decentralization. The other school, led most notably by Professor Yevsei G. Liberman of Kharkov University, does not deny the desirability of using computers to solve large-scale quantitative economic problems. But its adherents are skeptical that computer technology can keep pace with the demands that would be placed on it by an attempt to centralize all planning details. Instead they would rely on incentives that persuade lower-level decision makers to adopt policies coinciding with the planners' intentions.

The actual planning and management reforms announced at the September, 1965, Central Committee plenum and reaffirmed at the Twenty-third Party Congress, are heavily oriented towards the second, Liberman, school of thought. The goal of the changes has been summarized by Liberman himself:

> . . . to develop a system of planning and assessing the work of enterprises so that they will be vitally interested in the highest pos-

sible targets, in introducing new machinery and improving the quality of output, in a word, in the highest efficiency of production.[11]

The quotation diagnoses what is primarily wrong with the old planning system. The chief standard used to judge the performance of an industrial enterprise has been total gross output, subject to certain restrictions on its composition. The output indicator is supplemented by a multitude of secondary and frequently inconsistent ones—cost reduction, adoption of new techniques, labor inputs, to name a few—but the thirst for just plain more output has guaranteed the preeminence of the gross output target as the main criterion of enterprise success. To paraphrase Mr. Micawber: fifty kopecks over the plan, happiness; fifty kopecks under, misery.

The results are predictable. A lower plan target is more easily fulfilled; new techniques disrupt the production process, causing output to decline; and inferior goods are more easily produced in great quantities than superior ones. Moreover, enterprises are encouraged to use the most, not the least costly inputs, since purchase costs of materials are counted in gross output. Finally, buying firms have little control over selling firms because it is not easy to refuse substandard or incorrectly specified goods.

Liberman's proposal substitutes "profitability"—calculated as revenues less costs, divided by the firm's total assets—for gross output as the principal standard of performance. The firm must now sell its output to a willing buyer on a contractual basis to earn revenues. It will strive to reduce, not pad, input costs. And it will be encouraged to economize on its capital, heretofore used wastefully because it was granted free to the enterprise from the state budget or at a very low charge, usually two percent, from state banks. Gross output target fulfillment will still be a secondary indicator, but a graduated scale of bonuses and retention of earnings will encourage firms to set higher rather than lower targets.

The implementation of the planning changes is supposed to be gradual—only one-third of the industrial labor force was to have been employed in enterprises covered by the new scheme at the

[11] *Pravda*, September 9, 1962; translated in *Problems of Economics,* Vol. VIII, No. 3 (July, 1965), p. 3. A useful compilation of translations from the planning reform discussion is contained in *Problems of Economics* for June, July and August, 1965, and January, 1966.

end of 1966—although the pace will have to quicken if the original target date of complete changeover by January 1, 1968, is to be realized. A critical problem in the changeover is the nature of Soviet prices of industrial goods, which are notoriously unsound for economic purposes: a price of two rubles does not always represent twice as many resources as a price of one ruble. But for the Liberman type scheme to make sense, revenues and costs must be measured in prices reflecting the resources used. The necessity to adjust prices is explicitly recognized at top Soviet policy levels, but from all reports the two-year price "reform" currently underway seems to be mere tinkering with the old price structure rather than moving to a new one based on "opportunity cost" principles.[12] The question of prices is perhaps the single most dubious aspect of the new system of planning and management.

A note of caution: some foreign observers, along with several arch-reactionary Soviet economists and politicians, have read into the use of "profitability" a turn towards capitalism. However, the basic economic distinctions between Soviet style socialism and capitalism—concerning the forms of property ownership and the means of allocating resources—remain. Nowhere in the planning reforms is anything said about the State's selling off land and plant-and-equipment to individual Soviet citizens. Nor do the reforms abandon central planning; on the contrary, one of the motives for reform is to strengthen effective central economic control. In the words of one American observer, the reform is "an attempt . . . to season central planning with pinches of marketing and profiteering." [13] The official view of the changes is that "the market is to help fulfill the plan, not to replace the plan." [14] Professor Liberman and other Soviet economists have repeatedly made these two points in both the Soviet and Western presses, including a long letter by Liberman to *Time Magazine* in 1965.

Up to this point this study has been of the "supply" side of the Soviet economic growth problem, that is, at existing and possible future ways of organizing and supplying agriculture and industry.

[12] See Morris Bornstein, "Soviet Price Theory and Policy," in *New Directions in the Soviet Economy, op. cit.,* Part I, pp. 70, 77.
[13] Rush Greenslade, "The Soviet Economic System in Transition," in *New Directions in the Soviet Economy, op. cit.,* Part I, p. 13.
[14] *Ibid.,* p. 16.

The eighth five-year plan for 1966-1970 envisions increases of forty-seven to fifty percent in total gross industrial output (Soviet definition), and forty-nine to fifty-two percent in the gross output of capital goods—the sector of industry producing the "means of production" so crucial to future growth. Converted to annual average rates of increase, these figures work out to 8.0 to 8.5 percent and 8.3 to 8.8 percent respectively, substantially below those achieved even during the slowdown of 1959 to 1964 (9.2 percent and 10.4 percent [15]). If we assume that the proposed remedies for agriculture and industry will be successful, how can we account for such conservative targets for the growth of industrial output?

A major part of the answer lies on the "demand" side of Soviet growth possibilities. Two of the possible end uses of Soviet national income—improvements in the standard of living, including consumption levels, and outlays for defense and space—have received considerable attention in recent years. These two demands share the common feature of drawing resources away from uses productive of future growth.

### V. *The Soviet Standard of Living*

The privations of Soviet citizens were real enough in the early stages of industrialization: gross investment absorbed twenty to twenty-five per cent of the GNP—compared with twelve to fourteen per cent for the United States recently—and defense expenditures took out a further large chunk. When plan cutbacks had to be made, because of overoptimistic targets, Soviet planners consistently chose to trim consumer goods rather than capital goods and raw materials. What goods reached the shelves tended to be of unimaginative design and inferior quality. Housing conditions grew steadily worse from the beginning of the five-year plans in 1928 until just recently. Workers found their jobs hard and the workday lengthy. A progressive state policy on medical services and education only partially offset the grim lot of the Soviet man in the street.

---

[15] The former figure is from Table 2, (b), above. The latter is calculated from data in *Narodnoe khoziaistvo SSSR v 1964 g.: statisticheskii yezhegodnik* (National Economy of the USSR in 1964: Statistical Annual), Moscow, 1965, p. 124.

It is not surprising, then, that by the time of Stalin's death in 1953, the Russian people were ready for a break. In his "new course," Georgi Malenkov attempted to give them a small break by increasing the production of consumer durables, though they were relatively high in price, hence beyond the reach of the average worker. The "new course" never came to full fruition, but the point was not lost on Malenkov's successors: popular support could be won by paying more attention to consumer wishes.

By the late nineteen-fifties, greater quantities of consumer goods had begun to come onto the market, and Russian consumers responded eagerly—at first. But the "forgotten consumer's" first blush of demand for virtually *any* goods quickly faded, and by the early nineteen-sixties, the era of the "reluctant consumer" [16] had dawned. Inventories grew as consumers began saving more of their incomes; cartoons in the humor magazine, *Krokodil* (The Crocodile), belittled the lack of quality and sensitivity to the wishes of consumers in Soviet consumer goods—warehouses brimming with left shoes only, for example.

Soviet leaders responded by setting up research institutes for demand analysis and market forecasting. Economists wrote of planning consumer goods—involving fads and fickle tastes—as the most challenging task the planning system had yet faced and one which further increased the complexity of the economy and thus the pressure for reforming the planning system. To an older generation, these developments were a far cry from the ideals of the revolution; but surely, came the reply, the revolution would not be benefitted by filling warehouses with unsold merchandise.

Such is the setting of Premier Kosygin's report on consumer goods at the Twenty-third Party Congress.[17] First, the consumer goods industries are expected to grow by forty-three to forty-six percent (or 7.4 to 7.9 percent per annum on the average) over the five years 1966-1970, compared with only thirty-six percent for 1961-1965. Significantly, these industries, if the targets are achieved, will be growing almost as rapidly as the old favorite,

16 The phrase is Marshall Goldman's: "The Reluctant Consumer and Economic Fluctuations in the Soviet Union," *Journal of Political Economy,* Vol. LXXIII, No. 4 (August, 1965), pp. 366-380.

17 *Pravda* and *Izvestia,* April 5, 1966; translated in *Current Digest of the Soviet Press,* Vol. XVIII, No. 14 (April 27, 1966), pp. 6-7, 10.

heavy industry, whereas in the past the latter has always outpaced the former—for 1961-1965, on the average by 9.6 percent to 6.4 percent per annum. Also promised are higher quality and greater variety, hopefully according to the actual wishes of consumers instead of the guesses of planners. Is this to be Walt W. Rostow's stage of "high mass consumption?" Probably not yet, but major steps towards it appear in the offing.

Besides the quantity of consumer goods they can purchase, Soviet families are no doubt also interested in the amount of leisure time they have to enjoy these goods. It should be pointed out that the Soviet workweek and working day have never been so burdensome as those characteristic of capitalism in its early stages. Still, the workweek consisted of six eight-hour days until 1956, when it was reduced to a total of forty-one hours but still spread over six days.[18] A variety of promises has been made since 1956 to increase the leisure time of workers. The stated goal is to achieve a thirty-five-hour, five-day week by the "late nineteen-sixties," but a resolution of March, 1967, calls for a five-day week "retaining the present established duration of working time per week . . ."[19]— that is, forty-one hours. Unless the slackening of labor productivity growth is reversed, there will probably be a postponement of the thirty-five-hour week beyond 1970.

## VI. *Defense and Space*

The possibility of increased defense[20] spending poses perhaps the gravest threat to enhanced Soviet growth rates and consumption levels in the immediate future. Premier Kosygin intimated as much at the Twenty-third Party Congress in discussing Soviet aid to North Vietnam. Discounting the propaganda content of his state-

[18] See Arvid Broderson, *The Soviet Worker: Labor and Government in Soviet Society* (New York: Random House, 1966), *passim.;* this book is a convenient reference on the condition of the modern Soviet man-in-the-street.

[19] *Pravda* and *Izvestia*, March 15, 1967; translated in *Current Digest of the Soviet Press,* Vol. XIX, No. 11 (April 5, 1967), pp. 10-11.

[20] For simplicity of terminology, both defense and space are referred to simply as "defense." Both categories of outlays have military and other implications for international relations, and they require similar kinds of inputs (advanced scientists, special materials and equipment, large rocket engines), especially as the "post-nuclear" age of military technology advances.

ment, it would not be out of line with past experience if extra military outlays came at the expense of consumer goods and civilian producer goods—the proverbial "guns or butter" tradeoff.

The likelihood of a further Soviet arms buildup for Vietnam is outside the scope of this chapter. Presently available evidence suggests that the current level of defense spending does not severely strain the capacity of the Soviet economy.[21] Yet in a very real sense any defense spending at all entails a "burden" which is not fully offset by such civilian by-products as radar, heat resistant baking dishes and better weather prediction.

The burden of Soviet defense spending, as for any other nation, has three important economic aspects. First is its overall size in relation to national income. Budgeted defense outlays have been running on the order of seven or eight per cent of the "national income" (Soviet definition). Two difficulties arise: Soviet "national income" does not adequately reflect resource utilization, and not all defense expenditures are included in the budget item bearing that name. There have been several attempts by Americans to estimate the true total of Soviet defense outlays in relation to the Soviet gross national product (American definition).[22] Taking some liberties—for which the authors cited are not responsible—with these estimates, total defense spending is presently between twelve and fifteen per cent of GNP; the comparable figure for the United States is in the vicinity of ten per cent (although it may rise in 1967 if the costs of Vietnam continue to rise and the growth rate of GNP continues to slacken). These figures suggest a moderately greater relative defense burden on Soviet than on American resources, to be expected in view of the discrepancy between their GNP's, and the pressure on the Russians to keep at least within "hailing distance" of American defense capabilities.

The second aspect of the economic burden of defense spending is the composition of the expenditures. A large standing army

[21] L. C. Bloomfield, W. C. Clemens and F. Griffiths, *Khrushchev and the Arms Race* (Cambridge: MIT Press, 1966), especially chapters 3, 7 and 17.

[22] For example, Bloomfield *et al., op. cit.;* J. G. Godaire, "The Claim of the Soviet Military Establishment," in Joint Economic Committee, *Dimensions of Soviet Economic Power, op. cit.,* pp. 33-46; Abraham Becker, *Soviet Military Outlays since 1955,* RAND Corporation Memorandum RM-3886-PR, July, 1964.

draws away from the civilian economy resources far different in character from those taken by advanced missile systems. Recent Soviet—and American—defense policy has emphasized "fire power," delivered by planes and missiles, over personnel. Added to the space race, this has meant a large commitment of scientists, technicians and specialized production facilities. It is precisely those sorts of resources that could make the difference between success and failure in increasing productivity and efficiency in both industry and agriculture, and in expanding consumer goods output of high quality and wide variety. Premier Kosygin stressed shortages of scientific manpower in his Twenty-third Congress report on the new five-year plan.[23]

The third aspect of the defense burden is the effect on economic performance over time. Defense outlays are essentially a form of consumption: the more spent now, the lower the rate of investment; that means a lower rate of growth and a greater relative burden of given defense outlays in the future. This consideration must be uppermost in the minds of Soviet leaders as they ponder the implications of their commitments in Vietnam. The choice between winning the economic growth race against the United States and retaining the title of champion of world communism, would not be an easy one for them to have to make. Peking has not neglected to point out the "uncomradeliness" of the Soviet concern for domestic consumer goods while the North Vietnamese are losing their petroleum storage and electric power facilities.

## VII. *Summary*

The Soviet economy fifty years after the revolution is in a state of flux. Out of concern for a lagging rate of economic growth, Soviet leaders have initiated substantial changes in agricultural policy, and are midway to completion of a reform of industrial planning and management. At the same time they must juggle other goals which may well conflict with the goal of more rapid growth, principally demands for more consumer goods and better

[23] In terms of the growth race with the United States, of course, the American economy is subject to the same pressures. But it has a larger annual output, and whether the Vietnam war will offset this advantage and cause the United States to slip behind (or rather, less far in front) in the growth race is still an open question.

working conditions, and pressures for greater spending on defense and space projects.

But mere emphasis on change—certainly not a novelty in Soviet experience—is not enough if one is to gain some understanding of the direction and pace as well as the extent of the change. Keeping in mind the history of Soviet development over the past third of a century, particularly the years since World War II, this essay has viewed events in agriculture, planning and the standard of living as outgrowths of past policies: successful ones in the case of planning, not so successful in the other two. This does not mean that a simple extrapolation from the past will reveal the future course of economic affairs in the Soviet Union. One important variable that is especially hard to predict is the relative burden of the military budget. But hopefully this essay has provided a useful setting for evaluating further developments as they occur—as they surely will, and very likely at a rapid rate.

## Postscript, November, 1967

One of the main themes in the above article is that progress—or the lack of it—in Soviet agriculture would play a crucial role in determining future Soviet economic growth rates. If agriculture can expand, the rest of the economy can grow faster; if it cannot, it will exert a drag on other sectors such as industry.

The Brezhnev-Kosygin leadership has taken several positive first steps towards getting Soviet agriculture rolling: a doubling of planned state investments in agriculture for 1966-1970, as compared with 1961-1965, to forty-one billion rubles; substantial improvements in peasants' incentives to work harder in collective activities (rather than on their private plots); and a massive land reclamation and improvement program. The article took the position that these first steps would have to be followed up beyond 1970 by similar, perhaps yet greater ones, if more than a temporary uplifting of Soviet agricultural output and productivity were to be achieved.

Since the main text was completed, definite signs of shifts in agricultural policy have appeared. In a speech to the Supreme Soviet (the Soviet rubber stamp legislature) in October, 1967, top Soviet planner N. K. Baibakov announced a twenty-five percent reduction in planned state agricultural investments for 1966-1970. Instead of the original forty-one billion rubles, agriculture will have to make do with only some thirty billion—still a fifty percent increase over 1961-1965, but only one-half as great as the increase originally announced. At the same time, this bitter pill for agriculture was sweetened a bit by further improvements in incentives and working conditions, centering mainly on guaranteed incomes for collective farmers in collective activities, and retirement benefits.

On the basis of preliminary evidence, which is only fragmentary but nevertheless suggestive, one may tentatively outline the probable policy calculations by which the decision to cut back rather drastically on agricultural investments was reached. At the present time, the Russians want to expand consumer goods output and increase its quality, and to expand agricultural output in both foodstuffs and commercial products *and* to raise their quality as well, the while, maintaining the momentum in capital goods output that was built up and sustained from 1930 to the early nineteen-sixties. Their commitments in space, to their missile programs and (less important but still noticeable, and growing constantly) of supplies to their North Vietnamese allies must also weigh heavily in policy calculations.

Ideally, as would any nation, the Soviet Union would like to set and meet ambitious goals in all those spheres at once; presumably the initial computations for the eighth five-year plan (1966-1970) were predicated on realizing such high ambitions as nearly as possible. Evidently what has happened, as the second year of the plan nears its end, is that not all of the original goals can be met, and some cutbacks must be made. Agriculture has often in the past stood in line to no avail when scarce resources were being handed round, thus the present case is not a new departure. Apparently the ten or so billion rubles of state investments now to be freed from agriculture will be channelled into the consumer goods sector of industry—which, it is interesting to note, is scheduled to grow at a faster rate than the capital goods sector in 1968, for the first time since the "era of the plans" began in 1929.

There are some signs that the policy shift against agriculture in favor of consumer goods is a continuation of the longstanding feud within the Soviet leadership, noted in the main text of the article, between advocates and opponents of strengthening agriculture. The advocates, allied with Nikita Khrushchev from the late nineteen-forties until his removal (for "personal reasons") in October, 1964, and in the ascendant since late 1964, have apparently lost at least one round to their opponents. Thus, Party First Secretary Leonid Brezhnev, who came up in the Party under the aegis of Khrushchev, would like to see the agricultural program retained (and perhaps expanded). Government Premier Alexei Kosygin, on the other hand, is thought to favor strong expansion of consumer goods output, if necessary at the expense of agriculture. What this division (if it in fact exists) portends for the future of the Brezhnev-Kosygin regime, it is impossible yet to say. One can say, though, that at least for the moment there has been a de-emphasis of agriculture and a new emphasis placed on consumer goods output.

The arguments of the opponents of agricultural expansion must be premised on the belief that the Soviet economy, in spite of appearances to the contrary, can continue for some time to enjoy growth rates of five or six per cent per year without devoting as much investment to agriculture as originally envisaged in the Eighth Five-Year Plan. The counter premise of the Brezhnev group (with which the present writer is in basic agreement) is that it cannot. Developments in the coming years—unless the policy shift is soon reversed—will provide an empirical test to decide between the two competing hypotheses.

# 3

# Political and Economic Trends in Soviet Agriculture*

ROY D. LAIRD

ONE MAY or may not accept the assertion that failure in agriculture was the major factor behind Khrushchev's ouster in 1964, but there is little doubt that it was of enormous import.[1] This conclusion is supported by an imposing list of changes in agriculture that have been made and widely publicized since Khrushchev was removed from office. This list includes the following:

---

* An earlier version of the present paper was published in *Problems of Communism*, March-April, 1966, under the title "New Trends and Old Remedies."

[1] The argument that failures in the international arena were the major cause for Khrushchev's removal from office is surely far from the mark. Above and beyond the perspective of the agricultural problem outlined here, to credit foreign policy failures as most important is to fly in the face of the political axiom that foreign policy moves are almost inevitably an extension of domestic policies into the international arena. As important as the growing disintegration of the Communist world may have been (and failures there may well have furnished the final irritant that precipitated Khrushchev's ouster), surely the primary concern of the Soviet leaders must have been the serious slowdown in growth of the whole economy—industrial growth too was showing serious signs of lagging. True, the need to change from plan fulfillment to profit as the prime motivation for industrial growth was being increasingly discussed, but also more and more one could find candid remarks (starting with Stalin in his final years) to indicate that agriculture's lagging feet were increasingly retarding industrial growth as well.

---

Roy D. Laird is Professor of Political Science and Acting Chairman of Slavic and Soviet Area Studies at the University of Kansas.

1. the announcement of sharply increased agricultural investments, including significant increases in farm output prices, accompanied by a return to the old two-price system—i.e., base state prices for plan fulfillment, plus higher prices paid for state purchases of produce beyond plan,
2. the adoption of plans for significantly increasing the pace of draining marshlands and expanding the area under irrigation,
3. the encouragement of greater private plot production, primarily by cracking down on "illegal" restraints that had been placed on such operations,
4. the establishment of stable purchase plans for agricultural produce that are to remain unchanged throughout the new five-year planning period,
5. the removal of T. D. Lysenko from his central position in agricultural science and innovation,
6. the reinstatement of the Ministry of Agriculture as the dominant central agency of production administration,
7. the reestablishment of unified *rayon* (district) agricultural and industrial administrative agencies at the local level, and the parallel demise of Khrushchev's Territorial Production Administration,
8. the reinstatement of V. V. Matskevich as Minister of Agriculture and D. A. Kunayev as First Secretary of the Kazakhstan Party—men whom Khrushchev had tainted with the growing failure of his virgin lands scheme,
9. the promise to create a new Model Charter for Agricultural Artels,
10. the call for ending, for the foreseeable future, the transformation of *kolkhozy* into *sovkhozy* and for ending further amalgamation of farms into even larger units.

This is an imposing list, and the question arises, are there in these moves (plus other important modifications receiving less publicity) trends that portend significant changes on the Soviet agricultural scene? The answer to such a question cannot lie in an examination of the post-Khrushchev innovations alone. Indeed, any valid answer must be preceded by another question. In addition to the known, and serious, physical limitations, what is the base, the given, political-economic environment, that inevitably must shape and limit any innovation in the Stalinist agricultural system that the new leadership has inherited?

An understanding of current trends must start not only with a recognition that the Soviet system is a collectivized system comprised of *kolkhozy* (collective farms) and *sovkhozy* (state farms), but also with full appreciation that, although the Soviet Union is not the only modern state experimenting with large-scale collectivized agriculture, both the size of the Soviet farms and the administrative scheme which governs them are unique in history. The collectivized agricultural system is, perhaps, the most important of all of Stalin's questionable gifts to the Soviet system of rule; certainly it is the overriding feature of the Soviet rural scene. Thus an examination of the possible reasons for the costly creation of the Stalinist agricultural system in the first place surely is necessary, for in spite of many minor modifications in the nineteen-fifties and early nineteen-sixties, as of the fall of 1967 the Stalinist agricultural system remains essentially intact.

Why, in spite of the impressive revival of agricultural production under the NEP (New Economic Policy, 1921-1927), did Stalin impose forced collectivization on the infant Soviet society? The most obvious reason, although perhaps not the most important one, was the recognition that only agriculture could provide the enormous amounts of capital necessary for industrializing the Soviet Union at a forced draft pace. Some form of collectivization, therefore, seemed essential if the desired amount of capital was to be transferred from the farms to the factories. The second reason, less obvious but at least as important, was that the political situation at the end of the nineteen-twenties demanded the establishment of a collectivized system. Lenin and his followers had fully perceived that the 1905 revolution had aborted, because it lacked the organized support of the peasantry, who constituted the vast majority of the population. Later, having learned the lesson of 1905, the Bolshevik leadership became aware that the successes of both the 1917 Communist coup d'état and the subsequent civil war had depended upon peasant support—a joining of the agrarian and urban revolutions resulting from the peasants' attitude that given an unpleasant choice, they found the Bolsheviks the least repulsive of the various forces contending for political power. In view of the tenuous nature of the peasant-Bolshevik alliance, however, after the blood-letting was over, the potential of peasant power loomed ominously in Soviet politics. Therefore, although the NEP was aimed primarily at reviving industrial production, the new regime's leaders recognized that the mood of the countryside demanded a "peasant Brest-Litovsk." [2] Subsequently, though he ended the NEP, no one could have been more aware than Stalin in 1928 that the peasant masses had been the key factor shaping the establishment of Communist rule in Russia and that the peasantry remained by far the most important source of possible political— even revolutionary—opposition. Thus, the most important reason behind Stalin's "revolution from above" surely was the need to politically emasculate the peasantry. The risks involved in forcing the peasants onto the collectives were enormous, but once the *kolkhozy* were successfully established, and the machine tractor stations were created and placed firmly in control over the agricultural machinery as the major means of production, Marxist-Leninist rule was assured of a long tenure in the Soviet Union. [3]

Between the early nineteen-thirties and the beginning of the nineteen-fifties, little by way of significant economic or administrative innovation as such appeared in agriculture. Nevertheless, the Stalinist collectives gradually pressed the peasantry into a mold from which effective deviation became more and more impossible. True, the pace of change was radically increased by Khrushchev between 1953 and 1964 (actually beginning with the amalgamations of the collectives into even larger farms, which he initiated with Stalin's blessing in 1950), but even then no really fundamental change in the system occurred. True, Khrushchev destroyed Stalin's MTS (machine tractor stations), but this he could do in order to complete Stalin's "revolution from above." Although the dictatorship's iron grip over the countryside had long since been established, the focal point of the control over the collectives and

[2] David Ryabanov is credited with originating this description of the NEP. See, Merle Fainsod, *How Russia Is Ruled* (Cambridge: Harvard University Press, 1953), p. 97.

[3] If economic success is used as the primary yardstick, Professor Peter Wiles' arguments (presented in a seminar at The University of Kansas, July, 1965) that the achievements of the NEP rendered the adoption of centrally controlled planning and forced collectivization undesirable are most convincing (i.e., the rates of growth in both industry and agriculture prior to 1928 were significantly higher than afterwards). However, if the political imperative of the situation is taken into account, then Professor Alec Nove surely is correct in affirmatively answering his question, "Was Stalin Really Necessary." (The title article of a recent collection of his essays.)

state farms remained outside and above the farms. The seat of party direction was not in the *kolkhozy,* but in the MTS party units. Khrushchev, however, with additional reinforcements of party cadres from the cities, crowned his contribution to Soviet agriculture by transferring the party presence from the MTS to the farms—by 1958 virtually every farm had a party member chairman supported by a party unit, and the MTS became superfluous. Even on the less political side, Khrushchev's innovations contributed little in the long run towards advancing production. Increasing the number of specialists on the farms had perhaps the greatest impact,[4] and short-range advantages resulted from expanding the area in corn under the new lands and corn campaigns; but the 1955 decree on decentralized planning was almost completely ignored. Thus, as under Stalin apparently serious attempts were made through economic changes in the Khrushchev era to advance output, but political moves centered upon improving the system of controls predominated, often to the point of destroying economic gains that otherwise might have been enjoyed.

Finally, any examination of the rationale behind the Stalinist agricultural system must not ignore the theoretical determinants. As seen from the purely philosophical point of view, the introduction of Marxist communism into predominantly agricultural and peasant Russia was an anachronism. Therefore, the salvation of the souls of both the peasants and the leadership demanded some scheme wherein, just as in the case of the urban factory folk, the peasant farmers would enjoy a Communist relationship to the means of production. The *kolkhozy* and *sovkhozy* answered this ideological need. Beyond this, in the more practical realm of administrative theory, Lenin repeatedly argued for the superior path of adapting the industrial organizational pattern ("Communism equals the electrification of the countryside") to agriculture. Furthermore, closely related to the industrial administrative theory, but incorporating the mystique of the limitless expanse of Russian lands, was the conviction that hugeness of an enterprise somehow

[4] As discussed in Roy D. Laird, "The Dilemma of Soviet Agricultural Administration: The Short and Unhappy Life of the TPA," *Agricultural History,* Vol. XL, No. 1 (January, 1966), pp. 11-18; between 1953 and 1963 Khrushchev's efforts resulted in a more than doubling of the agricultural specialists working on the farms.

is equated with superior quality. Even Khrushchev, although he occasionally damned the excesses of "gigantomania," became caught up in the momentum of bigness, and thus presided over the severalfold increase in the size of the farms in his amalgamations. Thus the huge collective and state farms also fulfilled the demand to bring large-scale, industrial organization to the countryside.

Both the record of past achievements in agricultural production and the potential for success or failure of current and future agricultural policies must be weighed not only in such obvious terms as geographical influences and economic inputs, but also in the perspective of the history and belief system of the society and its leadership that produced the Stalinist *kolkhoz-sovkhoz* system with its political limitations and assets. Hopefully all of these factors will be allowed for here, but since, in this author's opinion, the importance of the political has been grossly shortchanged in the past this aspect of the problem will receive special attention.

Nearly one-half of Soviet society is still rural; most of this society lives and works in the huge *kolkhozy* and *sovkhozy* complex which comprises a unique system in the history of agriculture in their adoption of the industrial organizational pattern to the farms. Moreover, in the words of the Minister of Agriculture, agriculture is "the most extensive and complex branch of the Soviet economy." [5] Furthermore, the peasantry is recognized as the least integrated element of the society, and agriculture has remained the most serious domestic problem area. Clearly, political (using the broad sense of the term) factors vitally influence agricultural performance. Yet, in spite of the recent Soviet admission that agricultural production advances took a serious turn down between 1959 and 1965,[6] at a time when investment was on the increase, far too

[5] V. V. Matskevich, "Ekonomicheskie problemy dolneishevo razvitya sel'skovo khozyaistvo," *Voprosy ekonomiki,* No. 6 (June, 1965), pp. 1-13.

[6] The following is from the lead editorial of the April, 1965, issue of *Ekonomica sel'skovo khozyaistva,* pp. 1-9: "[T]he gross agricultural output during the Seven-Year Plan period (1959-1965) was supposed to have increased by 70 percent; in actuality in the six years it advanced only by 10 percent [and], it increased by only 1.9 percent in the last five years. . . . Thus, . . . the average grain yield rose . . . by only 0.8 centners during the period from 1960 to 1964. . . . In the last five years, . . . the number of hogs, sheep and poultry dropped considerably. On the average, the milk yield per cow dropped by more than 370 kilograms in the *kolkhozy* and *sovkhozy.*"

many argue that the Soviet agricultural production problem is almost entirely a matter of economies, and particularly of lagging investment. Thus, in the "imposing list of changes" summarized here earlier, only the greatly increased level of investment represents any fundamental change, and that not in the system itself. Perhaps the long delay in announcing the promised new Model Charter reflects a profound behind the scenes debate over the need for a fundamental organizational-administrative change, *but* the long silence is ominous.

Of course, the present observer may be very wrong in concluding that improved economic incentives alone will not alleviate the major production and efficiency shortcomings of Soviet agriculture. However, the following listing is a summary of some of the author's major observations resulting from past research. In essence the following represents assumptions concerning the peculiar political demands of Soviet agriculture that the Stalinist system has imposed upon agricultural production in the Soviet Union,[7] assumptions upon which the subsequent analyses of current changes and trends in Soviet agriculture rest.

1. New investments (including significant incentive increases) alone will not satisfactorily alleviate Soviet rural production ills. Ironically, although Khrushchev was never prepared to carry his reforms of the system far enough, his major emphasis on management problems was surely basically sound, whereas the first major actions of his successors (although they too stress administrative shortcomings) [8] can be taken as evidence that they may well emphasize the economic shortcomings at

[7] See, in particular, "The Politics of Soviet Agriculture," *Soviet Agricultural and Peasant Affairs*, Roy D. Laird, ed. (Lawrence, Kansas: The University of Kansas Press, 1963), pp. 269-86, "The Politics of Soviet Agriculture [continued]," *Soviet Agriculture: The Permanent Crisis*, Roy D. Laird and Edward L. Crowley, eds. (New York: Praeger, 1965), pp. 147-58, and "Khrushchev's Administrative Reforms in Agriculture: An Appraisal," forthcoming by the University of California Press in the collection of papers delivered before the August, 1965, Conference on Soviet and East European Agriculture.

[8] The resolution of the CPSU Central Committee that came out of the March, 1965, Plenary Session does assert that rectifying mistakes in agricultural management is "the most important task," (*Pravda*, March 27, 1965, p. 1) but, as the attempt shall be made to demonstrate, the balance of the new leadership's changes do not add up to a resolve to act in a manner implied by the use of such words.

the expense of equally fundamental administrative faults. Of course, *Soviet agriculture's problems will not be improved without serious economic reforms, but no amount of rubles expended can be expected, by themselves, to bring about the transformation of the administratively grotesque kolkhoz-sovkhoz system into an efficient production enterprise.*

2. Although there are social scientists in both the United States and the Soviet Union who study Soviet agriculture with a background understanding of agricultural problems, far too many analysts on both sides are city-born and bred. Ignoring the unique economic, social and political demands of the agricultural environment, they incorrectly assume, *a priori,* that the industrial revolution has had the same revolutionary impact upon agricultural production and the rural society that it has had on the urban factory setting. Such a point of view inevitably focuses only upon the new trees in the forest (e.g., tractors, combines and chemical fertilizers) and fails to perceive that, as impressive as these valuable new gadgets may be, the forest remains essentially unchanged—i.e., in essence, *the factory of agriculture is still the whole outdoors, an environment essentially dominated by the unharnessed forces of nature.*

3. Compounding the errors created by a view that the production process in agriculture has fundamentally changed, has been the *false assumption that the bureaucratic administrative system that is essential for efficient industrial production is also the best scheme for organizing and managing agricultural pursuits.* Thus, in the United States there is a widespread conviction that the so-called corporate farm has been increasing in import, when in fact the individual "manager-operated" farms seem to have shown the greatest production advances in recent years.[9] Similarly, in the Soviet Union, although Khrushchev often seemed to be genuinely working towards a greater decentralization of agricultural production decision-making, on balance his reforms strengthened outside controls over the farms. Moreover, as will be discussed in a later section of this essay, so far the new leadership also is giving top priority to controls, failing to see the conflicting size and management demands, if production efficiency is to be advanced.

4. As suggested in the preceding discussion, although increased

[9] See, for example, John J. Brewster and Gene Wunderlich, "Farm Size, Capital, and Tenure Requirements," *Adjustments in Agriculture: A National Basebook,* Carlton F. Christian, ed. (Ames, Iowa: Iowa State University Press, 1961), pp. 196-228.

economic investments in agriculture have been sorely needed, fundamental revisions in the system are needed even more. Given the ofttimes crucial factors of special local conditions, and the constant and often unpredictable alterations in the environment imposed by nature, the *successful farm manager needs the fullest freedom in production decision-making to respond to the ever changing demands of the plants and animals that he is nurturing.* Yet, to a degree greater than that in any other system in the world, the Soviet "on-the-farm" farm administrators are continually required to respond to outside, "above-the-farm," directives. True, Soviet observers do seem to see outside interferences as a serious fault, but the Soviet leadership has yet to make the changes necessary to end such practices.

Although the inherent blindspots of a totalitarian dictator are probably such that Khrushchev was unable to see the roots of many of his own failures in agriculture, surely he was not so blind as to fail to see that radically new courses of action were required, months before his ouster in October, 1964. Thus, for example, in response to the drought of 1963, Khrushchev called for a crash program to expand enormously the production of artificial fertilizers and other chemical aids. In fact there is good reason to conclude that he had already seen a portent of impending disaster at least a year earlier, for that was when he had created the Territorial Production Administration.

Traditionally, the Soviet leadership reacts to increased adversity by the hard line response of tightening controls. The year 1958 had been the peak of the post-Stalin production increases. The same year also brought the demise of the long-standing iron rule of the MTS over the countryside, and the beginning of timid experiments with greater freedom for the farms from outside controls. Very likely Khrushchev's perception that problems of agriculture were again mounting in 1962 was responsible for his creating the Territorial Production Administrations as a new arm of local production control. Indeed, in his call for establishing the TPA, he emphasized that with the abandonment of the MTS, too many comrades in the posts outside and above the farms had wrongly interpreted the move as a lessening of their responsibilities for successful production on the farms when in fact, he now asserted, they should have taken these responsibilities even more seriously.

Unfortunately, even though 1962 produced a relatively good harvest, 1963 brought the drought, and the Soviet Union found its grain reserves too low. Grain had to be purchased abroad, and the TPA hard line response was now recognized as inadequate. Thus, the much publicized chemical fertilizer campaign was started, and although it received most of the publicity, it was not the only important change underway. Publicly, Khrushchev also "dusted off" his call of several years earlier to emphasize the "production principle," instead of planning, as the prime measure of agricultural success. In essence, the "production principle" idea was to gauge achievement primarily on the basis of output of food per unit of land, rather than on plan fulfillment. Finally, although Khrushchev launched no public campaign to support the return to the *zveno* (some half dozen individuals working as "a team" or "link") as a desirable means of organizing the working groups on the *kolkhozy* (instead of the huge brigades, sometimes numbering over a hundred individuals), he surely must have tacitly encouraged the increasing number of articles appearing during his final years in office, articles that gave favorable mention to the *zveno* as a desirable basic work unit.

Full adoption of the *zveno* and the "production principle" surely would have resulted in profound changes in the collective farm system, but as in the case of the Stolypin reforms of over a half century earlier, actual changes in this direction were too little and, especially, too late to save the ruling Tsar. Just as in the case of Nicholas II, therefore, a failure to respond adequately to rural needs sealed the fate of Nikita S. Khrushchev.

Now Khrushchev is out, and the emphasis of the new leadership on plan fulfillment indicates that the "production principle" will be, at most, soft-pedalled and probably discarded.[10] Therefore, if there were a possible trend that could lead to the fundamental

[10] True, in his "Urgent Measures . . ." speech to the March, 1965, plenum, Brezhnev did assert that "the level of profitability must be placed at the base" of measuring the success of the farms, but in the Soviet Union (as elsewhere) one cannot have his cake and eat it too, and a move to "cost-accounting" principles on the farms is incompatible with stressing plan

changes that are needed in the system, the revival of the *zveno* remained the only visible hope.

The first major action of the post-Khrushchev leadership was to call a special party plenum on agriculture. Surely few Soviet citizens missed the significance of the single added work in the title of Brezhnev's major address to the March 24, 1965, special plenary session of the CPSU, which otherwise was identical with the title Khrushchev used for his own revolutionary admission of agricultural failures on September 3, 1953. Whereas Khrushchev's title had been "On Measures for the Further Development of Agriculture in the U.S.S.R.," Brezhnev's title was "On *Urgent* Measures for the Development of Agriculture in the U.S.S.R." [italics added.] [11]

Following the long standing conviction of the Soviet leadership that if only the management and leadership could be set right, the problems of agricultural production would be solved, both Brezhnev's March, 1965, speech and the subsequent party resolution did heavily stress administrative factors. Therefore, a first impression of a reader may well be that at long last a serious step will be taken to decentralize production decision-making. Now the farms will be given the freedom to respond freely to local conditions and needs. Unfortunately, the long history of advancing centralization in agricultural administration, plus the stress key officials have given the changes introduced by the new leadership will not support such an optimistic conclusion.

Hope that a new trend might be towards greater "on-the-farm" autonomy in production decision was supported by a move that occurred even before the special March plenum. Khrushchev's TPA were shorn of their party committees in November of 1964. However, the March, 1965, move to dismantle the rest of the Khrushchev administrative apparatus included the re-creation of all too familiar control agencies. Indeed, if described in chart

---

fulfillment as the most important of all factors. See "O neotlozhnykh merakh po dol'neishemu razvitiyu sel'skovo khozyaistva SSSR," Doklad . . . L. I. Brezhneva . . . 24 Marta 1965 godu, *Sel'skaya zhizn'*, March 27, 1965, pp. 2-4.

[11] *Ibid.*

form, while fulfilling the need to employ a kind of spoils system to a one party state,[12] agricultural administration has been returned to much the same form that existed prior to 1958, but without the MTS.[13]

As subsequently outlined by Minister of Agriculture, V. V. Matskevich, the Union Republic Ministry of Agriculture (including some forty-three main administrations, commissions and associations which are responsible for almost every conceivable aspect of agricultural activity)[14] has been reinstated as the focal point of production control and direction over counterpart ministries in the various republics. Below the republic ministries the *oblast* (or regional) administrations are to continue as major sources of administrative control, specifically charged with being responsible for "operational direction" (*operativenoe rukovodstvo*) of the farms. Finally, although somewhat fewer in number than they were in the late nineteen-fifties, the *rayon* administrations, directly supervised by the *oblast* agencies and immediately over the farms, have been resurrected and are again described as powerful agencies, now responsible for "working out problems of placing orders for production and delivery" of state purchases, "distributing funds for

[12] The penchant for Soviet leaders to change administrative schemes at the time of important changes in the configuration of the top leadership obviously reflects a dissatisfaction with old administrative relationships. However, the present observer increasingly has become convinced that another important factor is responsible for the constant reorganization of Soviet administration. Most of the people in key posts at the time of Khrushchev's ouster must have felt that they owed their positions directly, or at least indirectly, to him. With a sweeping reorganization, however (and even though most of the old bosses are reappointed to new posts of importance), those in the new hierarchy of command will have a feeling that they owe their positions to the new leadership. In short, the Soviet administrative system seems to have adapted the essence of the Jacksonian spoils system to a one party state.

[13] Perhaps not even without the MTS, for noting that the "repair base" was "seriously undermined" when the MTS were dismantled, Brezhnev not only called for improvement in this realm, but specifically asked for "the creation of mechanized detachments and machine-rental, mechanized animal husbandry and meadow-reclamation stations for the fulfillment of various specialized jobs. . . ." See, *Pravda*, March 27, 1965, *op. cit.*

[14] "V ministerstve seliskovo khozyaistra SSSR." *Kolkhozno-sovkhoznoye proizrodstvo*, No. 8, 1965, pp. 47-48.

equipment and construction, . . . [and] rendering day-to-day assistance to the farms in solving complex problems." [15]

Perhaps, at long last there will be "a resolute turning away from
the practice of administration and the command and replacement
of the managers and specialists of the *kolkhozy* and *sovkhozy*" on
the part of the higher authority.[16] However, production failures
result in failures to fulfill plans and Matskevich's own words (in a
discussion of the "Economic Problems of the Further Development
of Agriculture") are that the responsibility for the "operational direction" given the *rayon oblast* (*krai*) and republic administrations
means that the "fulfillment of the [State] plan for purchases . . .
be guaranteed. . . ." [17] Perhaps central leadership will no longer
attempt to impose itself upon the day-to-day production administration of the *kolkhozy* and *sovkhozy* as did Khrushchev, but
the practical separation of the responsibility for planning, the assur-
ance of delivery, and the direction of production, is surely impossible. Perhaps the orders may now emanate from republic or
*oblast* officers but such offices are just as much out of touch with
immediate local needs as are offices located in Moscow. In this
regard, the Minister of Agriculture goes to great pains to spell out
that the *rayon* administrations are responsible for seeing not only
that planned state purchases are "unquestionably fulfilled," but
also that "possibilities for above-plan . . . purchases . . . are fully
utilized. . . ." Further elaborating on the responsibility of the *rayon*
organizations, Matskevich asserts that they "must carefully examine the plans given to them [by the farms], and if necessary make
corrections, and only after this, confirm the individual plans for
each *kolkhoz* and *sovkhoz,* but with the understanding that the
state purchases for the *rayon* be fulfilled *unquestionably*" [italics
added].[18] Surely the whole history of the system cries that no

[15] "Na uroven' novykh zadach," *Selskaya zhizn!* June 24, 1965, p. 2. As
of early 1965 in the Ukraine and the RSFSR alone, some 1,945 unified
urban rural *rayon* administrations had been established (see, *Pravda,* February 6, 1965, p. 2, and *Izvestia,* January 16, 1965, p. 4) and by the March
plenum, Brezhnev announced that some 2,434 *rayon* party committees had
been created (*op. cit.*).

[16] *Ibid.*

[17] *Voprosy ekonomiki,* No. 6, June, 1965, *op. cit.*

[18] *Ibid.*

ambitious *rayon* secretary can resist giving production orders to the farms under his command.

Soviet commentary has stressed that the combination of establishing stable, unchanging procurement plans for the 1966 to 1970 planning period, and increasing state investments during the period to sixty-two billion rubles (assertedly nearly the equal of the total investment in agriculture during the first nineteen post-war years),[19] must be reflected in increased production. The promised new investments are impressive, and, *if implemented,* they should produce new levels of output, but if at least half of the problem is political and administrative, the rewards reaped from increased peasant incentives and new aids and equipment alone are bound to be disappointing.

Before Khrushchev ended the old two-price system, Western observers agreed that it had distorted incentives, yet one of the new leadership's solutions is to go back to the old scheme of higher prices for above plan sales to the State. More than this, there is already the hint that the asserted voluntary, above plan sales will increasingly come to be regarded as mandatory.[20]

Beyond the above key economic changes, illegal restrictions on private plot production (apparently encouraged by Khrushchev in his latter years in office) are to be stopped; the impossible debts of many of the more backward collectives (accrued largely as a result of their purchases of MTS equipment) are to be canceled; large, new drainage and irrigation projects are to be undertaken; credits to farms for improvements are to be eased; and a new, more liberal tax on net (rather than gross) farm income is to be adopted.

In total, the promises for improvement in the economic realm are impressive and, if fully implemented, probably do constitute a new trend in agriculture, or at least a return to the higher investment policies practiced by Khrushchev in his early years in power.

[19] Brezhnev, *Pravda,* March 27, 1965, *op. cit.*

[20] The lead editorial of *Ekonomica sel'skovo khoziaistva,* No. 4 (April, 1965), pp. 1-9, carries the statement that "initially" above plan purchases will be made on a "voluntary basis" without assignment of above the plan sales obligations.

[21] See, Roy D. Laird, "Soviet Agricultural Output in 1980: An Appraisal," *Ost Europa Wirtschaft,* No. 2 (June, 1965), pp. 90-104.

Nevertheless, as concluded earlier in a published analysis of potential advances that might come from economic reforms alone, this author's prediction still stands, that the Soviets can be expected to remain a net importer of food (at least of the key commodity, grain) for several years to come. The Brezhnev-Kosygin economic program provides no new reason for altering such a conclusion.[21] Although the post-Khrushchev leadership has exhibited a clear resolve to turn over a new leaf in the realm of agricultural economic practices, there is as yet no clear indication that this trend is to be matched by innovation on the administrative side of the coin. The administrative problem of Soviet agriculture is rooted in the unwieldy size of the huge farms themselves. By 1965 there were some 11,681 *sovkhozy* (averaging some 7,600 sown hectares and some 2,100 cattle, including 780 cows with some 660 workers), and 36,300 agricultural *kolkhozy* (averaging some, 2,800 sown hectares and some 900 cattle, including 300 cows with some 610 workers).[22] Perhaps the 1964 promise to create a new *kolkhoz* charter does carry with it an implicit resolve to dismantle the *kolkhoz-sovkhoz* system in practice, if not in name, but that promise has as yet to be fulfilled. As implied earlier, the only activity that has given real promise of meeting the dire need for fundamental reorganization of agricultural administration was the publication of a series of successful experiments in breaking up the huge farms into *zveno* units, but these experiments now seem to be condemned. This, in spite of the inauguration in the mid-nineteen-sixties of studies of optimum farm size and Brezhnev's assertion that some of the present farms are "so large that they have proved to be unmanageable." [23]

Accounting for variations in types of farms, findings of American studies on farm size and management indicate that within a given type of farm, beyond certain limits of size, efficiency of operation begins to fall. True, American farms vary considerably in size according to the type of operation, and the size of the average farm (i.e., some 120 hectares—300 acres—in 1959) continues to grow. Nevertheless, whatever the setting, the optimum

[22] *Narodnoe khozyaistvo SSSR v 1965 godu*, Moscow, 1966, pp. 257, 405 and 425.

[23] *Pravda*, March 27, 1965, *op. cit.*

size of the most efficient farm must be closer to the American average, since the average American farmer consistently produces much more than his Soviet counterpart in a situation wherein (in 1959-1960) there were some sixty-one farm hectares per American farm worker as contrasted with some thirteen farm hectares per farm worker in the Soviet Union (in 1964).[24] Moreover, such studies probably have universal application. Certainly, data gathered by the author in Poland during 1967 clearly indicates that the smallest of the Polish state farms are much more efficient than the largest of such Polish farms—and these farms are many times smaller than the average Soviet collective and state farms. This then gives a measure of import of the *zveno* as a basic unit of organizing the peasants in their work activities. Indeed, the past literature on the *zveno* indicates that where successful experiments with these teams have been made, although the *kolkhozy* nominally remain intact, in fact the collectives involved are broken up into smaller farms managed by some half dozen or so individuals. For example, V. Zhulin, Chief Agronomist of the Krasnoyarskiy Sovnarkhoz, Altayskiy Krai, describes the successful *zveno* as follows:

> In order that a team be on the land as *an active owner, the land should be a legal assignment, not a conditional one.* [italics added.] A team has to be of four to six persons. . . .

> A team that enters a *kolkhoz* or *sovkhoz* as a primary production unit must have a single will . . . subordinated . . . to the authority of the detachment leader. . . .[25]

Unfortunately, for the hope for such a change, Stalin, quite correctly from the Communist point of view, condemned Politburo

[24] These calculations are based upon statistics presented in *Agricultural Statistics 1963*, United States Department of Agriculture, Washington, 1963, pp. 433-34 and 448, where it is reported that in 1959 there were some 1,120,158,000 acres (one acre = 2.45 hectares) of land on all American farms, 3,703,894 farms, and the average number of individuals employed in farm work between 1956-60 was some 7,500,000. The Soviet farm size and area figures are cited above (*ibid.*) and in *SSSR v tsifrakh v 1964 godu:* Moskva, 1965, pp. 93 and 94, where it is reported that in 1964 the average number of workers per *sovkhoz* was 717 and that there were a total of 15,900,000 *kolkhoz* households (the present calculations assume an average of two workers per household, implying some 32,000,000 *kolkhoz* workers).

[25] *Komsomol'skaya pravda*, August 7, 1965, pp. 1-2.

member Andreyev in the late nineteen-forties, for championing the *zveno* as the most efficient means of organizing production work. The *zveno* members undoubtedly did tend to evolve separatist attitudes towards their collectives—tending to regard the fields and animals under their charge as personal property. On the other hand, Andreyev surely observed correctly that these teams, which had grown in importance during the relatively relaxed controls during the War, had proved to be much more efficient production units than the large brigades.

Agriculture in the late nineteen-forties was in serious trouble, it was not living up to expectations economically or politically. In a real sense, then, Stalin was faced with the choice of following Andreyev's course, one that on the record promised greater production but at the expense of tighter controls, or the alternative offered by Khrushchev in his amalgamations which assured greater controls but contained no real proof that production would be increased. Indeed, Khrushchev's course not only promised increased controls as such, but it also incorporated the continued maximization of capital transfer from the countryside to the cities (so that "all priority to industrial construction" could be maintained). Furthermore, it promised the capture of the collectives by the Party at long last, and thus the completion of Stalin's "revolution from above," by fully incorporating the farm leadership into the direct hierarchy of rewards and punishments that extends from Moscow to the local production unit.[26] As a result, the *kolkhoz* peasantry and their activities—with the important exception of their private plot enterprises—are now fully encompassed in the single administrative pyramid that envelops virtually every human being and nearly all human activity in the Soviet Union.

Thus, for control reasons Stalin outlawed the *zveno*. Article after article appeared in the Soviet press in a questionable attempt to prove that the huge brigades constituted a superior production form. In the late years of Khrushchev's rule, however, a quiet

[26] True, the farm chairman's income still depends upon the success of the farm, but the balance of his rewards and punishments (e.g., promotion to a higher place), since he is now a party leader, is as fully linked to Moscow as long since has been the case with the factory manager—after all, even the factory manager's level of income depended to a large degree upon his bonuses for "fulfilling and overfulfilling plan."

reversal became apparent. Articles, including some in the "School of Agriculture" series in the important weekly, *Ekonomicheskaya gazeta,* were published praising the effectiveness of the *zveno* in various operations.[27]

Unfortunately, for the future of Soviet agriculture—and for the future health of the whole Soviet economy—the *zveno* movement has been the only visible path for solving the political-administrative ills of Soviet agriculture. Yet, an assertedly scientific comparative study, made by the Ukrainian Agricultural Academy, has been published as proof of the superiority of the brigades over the *zveno*[28] and new charges that the *zveno* "represent a falacious, nonsocialist path"[29] lead to the conclusion that the new Soviet leadership is not as yet prepared to look seriously at the ills of the *kolkhoz-sovkhoz* system.

Grain is far and away the most important crop in the Soviet Union. Fortunately, the weather in 1966 was excellent for this crop and the best harvest ever was gathered. Although obviously not as good as in 1966, available reports indicate that the weather in 1967 was generally favorable, and another good grain crop was harvested. Apparently the coincidence of good weather and the inauguration of the new investments in agriculture have created an optimism in the minds of the current leadership that the major problems of food production have been solved. Such, at least, is an attitude reported by recent visitors to the Soviet Union. Unfortunately, however, beyond a history of good and bad crop years the problems discussed here lead to a conclusion that until major political reforms are undertaken in the countryside, agriculture can be expected to remain the major Soviet domestic problem area.

[27] See, for example, "Organizatsiaya truda v kolkhozakh i sovkhozakh," *Ekonomicheskaya gazeta,* No. 5 (February 1, 1964), pp. 1-6 of insert.

[28] V. Borovsky, *Ekonomika sel'skovo khozyiastvo,* No. 10, 1965, pp. 37-51.

[29] A. Strelyany, *Komsomol'skaya pravda,* October 15, 1965, pp. 2-3.

# 4

## Young Soviets and an Aging Komsomol

### WILLIAM M. JACKSON

FIFTY YEARS ago the October Bolshevik Revolution brought a new order to Russia and the territories that make up the Soviet Union. The next half century brought the Soviet people great hardships, but also many achievements. On their fiftieth anniversary the Soviet Union could boast not only of their space exploits but also of a massive, modern educational system and an economy that is increasingly giving the Soviet people the necessities and luxuries they desire.

And yet those who are to benefit the most from the Soviet Union's achievements—those who did not directly suffer the hardships of collectivization and rapid industrialization—have become one of the government's major problems. Over half the Soviet population is under twenty-six years of age. Soviet children, we are often told with a smile, are "our only privileged class"—and this is largely true. But in the past year the official Communist party youth organization—the Young Communist League, or *Komsomol* —has had to launch a "checkup" of its own ranks and an intensified ideological campaign to convince youth of the value of communism. Furthermore, it has called for a similar ideological campaign for its ward, the Pioneers—a twenty-three million member

William M. Jackson is a researcher and writer with the Institute for International Youth Affairs, New York, in Soviet youth affairs and the international Communist youth and student fronts.

organization enveloping virtually all Soviet children from ten to fifteen.

*Komsomol,* which was founded in 1918, encompasses well below half the youths within the eligible age group of fourteen to twenty-eight. Self-avowedly an offspring of the Communist Party of the Soviet Union (CPSU), its purposes are basically to help instill in *all* Soviet youths the ideology of Marxism-Leninism as interpreted by the CPSU; to provide the Party with a mechanism for organizing vast numbers of youths for various projects, particularly economic ones; to forestall the possibility that youth might form non-party organizations by feeding them into a ready-made, and obedient, youth organization; to serve as a training ground for future leaders of Soviet society. The Pioneers' program involves similar ideological goals, and also includes some economically and socially useful work projects, but it places more emphasis on recreational pursuits. The only other youth organization is the Octobrists, for children from seven through nine years of age.

While at its Fourteenth Congress in 1962 *Komsomol* had been able to address itself primarily to mobilizing youths for the regime's economic projects, at its Fifteenth Congress in May, 1966, economic tasks were largely pushed aside. The organization had to make up for losses in its ideological program. Its leadership function, too, had diminished, as fewer party members than ever were being recruited from *Komsomol* ranks. Moreover, signs were increasing that Soviet youths were less interested in *Komsomol* than ever, that they were too busy joining the twentieth century to occupy themselves with the old, dull puritanism of early revolutionary heroes that *Komsomol* was preaching. While *Komsomol* claims a membership of twenty-three million, indications are that twenty million Soviet people go dancing—at clubs, homes and parties—every night.[1]

Within about a year *Komsomol* launched three basic programs in a two-pronged attack designed to steel youth ideologically and to develop the activism of *Komsomol* members. The ideological program was given the go-ahead at a *Komsomol* Central Commit-

[1] *Komsomolskaya Pravda* (hereafter referred to as *KP*), Moscow, April 20, 1967.

tee plenum in December, 1965, and formally ratified as *Komsomol's* program for the next four years by the Fifteenth Congress. Dedicating itself to "educating youth in the revolutionary, labor and fighting traditions of the Soviet people and of the Communist party," [2] the Congress envisioned a spate of measures designed to implement their teaching program: various military-patriotic educational programs, special writing prizes for literary works esteemed by *Komsomol* officials, celebrations of a young worker's first payday, history and ideology discussion clubs, cultural circles, in-school and out-of-school propaganda, ideological-political training circles in factories. To improve their image among members and non-members it was proposed that local *Komsomol* branches record their own histories and that members press for more material on *Komsomol* in school textbooks. In honor of the Soviet Union's fiftieth birthday a nationwide contest for the best student work on *Komsomol* or the international youth movement was organized.

The second program was organizational. The Fifteenth Congress reversed a rule made at the previous Congress limiting the number of consecutive terms a *Komsomol* functionary could serve; this was done because too many inexperienced youths had taken leadership positions in *Komsomol* branches. Also designed to improve the quality of *Komsomol* work was the new rule that people recommending prospective members for *Komsomol* be kept responsible for the performance of those they recommend. Furthermore, those applying for membership are to be given assignments as a test of their devotion and capability. By far the most ambitious part of the program is the renewal of *Komsomol* membership cards, or the "checkup of the social activeness of everyone entering *Komsomol*." The first reissuing of cards in twelve years, it serves a dual purpose—in the words of the resolution: "To further tighten up discipline and organization in the *Komsomol* and re-

[2] Reports and resolutions of the Fifteenth Congress were published in *KP*, May 18-22, 1966, and in *XV S"ezd Vsesoyuznogo Leninskogo Kommunisticheskogo Soyuza Molodezhi, 17-21 Maya 1966 godu, Stenograficheskii Otchet*, Moscow, 1966. Unless otherwise stipulated *Komsomol* statistics cited in this paper were from the Congress material.

move the shortcomings in *Komsomol* registration," i.e., to find out just how many members really are in the organization.

Shortly after starting the checkup *Komsomol* initiated a third campaign which combined the ideological and organizational purposes of the first two. The *Komsomol* Central Committee at a plenary session in the beginning of February, 1967, pledged to improve *Komsomol* leadership of the Pioneers. The ideological program called for "cultivating in the Pioneers a love for the Soviet Army; improving their training in the defense of the Socialist Fatherland, and imbuing the children with such qualities as courage, selflessness and filial devotion to the homeland." The military portion of the program was especially emphasized, and Sergei Pavlov, First Secretary of *Komsomol,* complained, "We have not yet been able to find sufficiently effective means to stimulate and encourage the desire of youngsters to engage in applied military forms of sports." Just over two months later a new Pioneer statute was published declaring as basic ideological objectives fealty to the familiar "revolutionary, fighting and labor traditions of the Soviet people." The school would remain the basic center of Pioneer activity, though *Komsomolites* might also pursue the Pioneers to their homes. Hobby clubs, scientific societies and communal activities are among the less political Pioneer activities. Among the more crucial rules from *Komsomol's* point of view is the one that stipulates that "the Pioneer prepares himself to become a member of *Komsomol.*" [3]

These programs were born from the desire of *Komsomol,* and the Party beyond it, to assert their control over the young generation which has been increasingly in the grip of powerful social forces. Since the end of World War II, and especially since Stalin's death, the Soviet Union has made seven league strides to join the industrialized elite of the world. Automation and cybernetics, mass production and mass communications, the capacity for nuclear war and for peaceful prosperity—these have produced tensions in all industrialized nations of the postwar world.

[3] Second *Komsomol* Plenum, February, 1967: Resolution in *KP,* February 5, 1967; Pavlov's report in *KP,* February 3, 1967; Pioneer Statute in *KP,* April 19, 1967.

Juvenile delinquency is on the increase. "In certain regions and cities law violations on the part of juveniles are growing," a recent Soviet Supreme Court resolution stated,[4] and that it may even have minimized the problem was evident from several party and state decrees designed to deal with juvenile delinquency, hooliganism and crime in general that were passed from July to September, 1966. Along with other Soviet cities, Moscow has been bothered by juvenile incidents for years, one of the most publicized having been the "rumble" on Red Square between two graduating classes in June, 1965, which resulted in one death. At the start of 1966 a curfew was issued in Moscow to get schoolchildren off the streets by 10:00 p.m. Juvenile violence is not the West's monopoly, as was illustrated by *Izvestia's* coverage of a juvenile extension of an official campaign to kill stray dogs and cats:

> We write in such detail about the goings-on in Kerch where thousands of registered and taxed cats and dogs were shot, because we see this and similar actions as a possible cause of the meaningless cruelty rampant among teenagers today. The youngsters, just like the Kerch town officials, feel that despite the protests of the enraged pet-owners and general public, they can mutilate and kill animals with impunity. Being subject to a kind of psychological instability, some teenagers are trying to repeat the sharp sensation experienced during the official butchering of cats and dogs.[5]

Other aspects of modern living are also troubling the Party. In the past few years several proposals have been made in the Soviet press about teaching sex at schools. This reflects serious concern about the number of abortions (one of the Soviet Union's most available and inexpensive forms of birth control). The "sexual revolution" seems to have come to the Soviet Union. One survey of Leningrad higher educational students showed that over half the men approved of pre-marital sexual relations, as did over one-third of the women. Those interested in teaching youth a "mature" attitude toward sex were starting with a handicap, however: a study of ninth graders in the Lithuanian capital of Vilnius showed that

[4] *Sovetskaya Yustitsiya*, No. 21, 1966.
[5] *Izvestia*, undated—Translated by *New Statesman*, March 18, 1966, London.

only six per cent learned the facts of life from their parents while the rest learned from friends or questionable literature. When separate pamphlets on sex were issued, the boys and girls traded pamphlets with each other. The government's publishers have not revealed a particularly mature attitude either. Their standard book on the subject, *Boy and Girl,* resorts to invoking the specter of venereal disease in hopes of steering youths away from sex, as well as the ideological argument that men who seek to become Don Juans "will never make good Communists."

Divorce is increasing and officials predict that it will continue to increase for a number of years. Furthermore, a major cause of divorce, as of crime, is the old Russian problem of alcohol. And "firm steps to eradicate drunkenness have still not been taken," one party official has complained.[6] This is true in rural areas, too, where a recent study has shown that doubled earnings have been accompanied by doubled vodka sales and a lowering of work discipline and "communist psychology." Bad manners, a snobbish attitude toward physical labor, elitist tendencies (students in one case even had the affront to demand that a worker eating in a restaurant give them his table [7])—all these are signs of new times.

Other, more positive, signs of modern times also affect Soviet youths—a high level of education, striving for technological skills, ambition for highly placed and challenging jobs, a desire to see and know the world, the thrill of participating in the adventure of building their country and, as they are told, a new society. Hundreds of thousands of young Soviets have braved harsh conditions taming the far North and East—though perhaps more for the adventure, the romance, the responsibility, even the extra pay than because the Party ordered it. But they have gone, and are still going; and even if they return from the frontier after only a year or two they have made their contribution. Others study, learn skills, advance in their jobs. These far outnumber the juvenile delinquents. They do, nevertheless, concern the Party, for even if they are highly motivated to act for the good of society, or even if their selfish desires motivate them to be good workers and solid citizens, the Party basically wants them to act for the good of the Party.

[6] *Izvestia,* January 4, 1967.
[7] *Izvestia,* November 11, 1966.

The Party is concerned about the future effects of petty anti-social acts on society and perpetuating its social and political control.

Just over ten years ago, however, the Party itself was compromised. With the exposure of Stalin's sins the myth of infallible leadership was exploded. Soviet youths have not been brought up in the same unquestioning tradition as many of their elders; for eleven years the knowledge that the supreme Soviet leader was often criminally wrong has matured. One result is an increasing scepticism of functionaries, that has, among other things, weakened *Komsomol's* hold over Soviet youth and Soviet youth's tolerance of ideological and bureaucratic platitudes. This, however, has not necessarily weakened their devotion to the broad ideals they attribute to communism—equality, material well-being for all, justice.

If Soviet behavior has been altered by industrialization and its obedience tested by de-Stalinization, there is the possibility that a major blow to Soviet faith in Communist ideals will be dealt by the present Sino-Soviet split. The present militarization campaign in the Soviet Union may have been developed as the war in Vietnam escalated, but it has been broadly intensified as Soviet-Chinese relations worsened. It is now clearly geared to China, whose military threat and whose challenge to the supremacy of the CPSU in the world Communist movement may turn Soviets back in on themselves. The doctrine of coexistence, the development of polycentrism in the Communist movement and increased Soviet-American amity can hardly foster militant Communist internationalism. Nationalism, self-interested trade with the West, hostility toward other Communist countries may cause deeper marks on future Soviet citizens than can be neutralized by the ideological education program.

The major national trends of industrialization and de-Stalinization and the international trend towards polycentrism, therefore, surely influence Soviet youth more than the values promulgated by the press, schools and the youth program.

It is quite evident that Soviet youth is not the same as the official *Komsomol*, although *Komsomol* does include a large number of young Soviets between the ages of fourteen and twenty-eight. *Komsomol* First Secretary Pavlov claimed in 1965 that there were nearly seventy million Soviet citizens between the ages of fourteen and thirty.[8] With this figure as a base—and Pavlov's authority as well as other estimates of the Soviet population indicate that it is a valid figure—it can be estimated that *Komsomol's* twenty-three million members represent less than forty percent of the total possible membership. This proportion sharply contrasts with the Pioneers which, Pavlov reported two years later, include "all schoolchildren from ten to fifteen years of age." [9] There are thus twenty-three million children in the five-year Pioneer age group, as compared with twenty-three million *Komsomolites* in the fourteen-year *Komsomol* age group.

A general picture of *Komsomol* members shows that approximately one-quarter are students. The organization has been growing younger, and at the Fifteenth Congress Pavlov reported that the number of members between fourteen and seventeen had risen sharply and that the proportion of *Komsomolites* between eighteen and twenty-five had decreased by twenty-three percent. Although this is partially a result of the World War II's effect on the Soviet birthrate and also of *Komsomol's* lowering of its minimum age limit from fifteen to fourteen, it is also due to a significant attrition of older *Komsomolites*. Between 1962 and 1966 fifteen million new members entered the organization. Even accounting for the loss of four year's worth of members who passed beyond the age limit and for *Komsomol's* growth by 3.6 million members (part of which was the effect of the lowered minimum age), between a third and a half of those fifteen million apparently just dropped out of the organization. Indeed, probably more have dropped out as the twenty-three million membership figure has recently been called into question: "The large movement of youth around the country . . . plus existing deficiencies in conducting the *Komsomol* registration has led to the fact that a certain number of *Komsomol* members have left *Komsomol* without being struck off the register and have proven to be outside the organization." [10] Yet another indication of a fairly extensive lack of members' concern is non-payment of dues. Despite the fact that membership dues have been

[8] *Partiinaya Zhizn*, No. 5 (March, 1965).
[9] *KP*, February 3, 1967.
[10] *KP*, October 12, 1966.

reduced by over half at the past two Congresses, *Komsomol's* business manager recently complained that "in many organizations membership dues had become a purely symbolic act." [11]

The gap between *Komsomol* and youth is reflected in a gap between *Komsomol* rank and file and *Komsomol* leaders, whose primary allegiance is to the Party, not youth. There are quite a few party people now in *Komsomol's* upper echelons as can be seen from a look at those selected to attend the Fifteenth Congress. Of the 3,821 delegates, twelve were deputies of the Supreme Soviet of the Soviet Union and 512 were deputies of republican or local Soviets; 666 were members of elected party organs, and 2,306, or sixty percent of the delegates were members or candidate members of the Party (a slight increase from the 1962 Congress). Pavlov, of course, is the Party's highest emissary to *Komsomol* and is a member of the CPSU Central Committee.

While *Komsomol* had grown younger, the leadership had grown much older. Aside from the aging Pavlov (born in 1929), one-quarter of the delegates were twenty-nine or over. At the 1962 Congress 292 (of a total 3,862) delegates were twenty-nine to thirty; in 1966 there were 589 delegates in this age group. In 1962, 259 delegates were over thirty; in 1966, 371 were over thirty.[12] No statistics were given for the number of delegates twenty-eight or over, although it is believed that a large number of functionaries stay beyond their twenty-eighth birthday, as is permitted by the statute.

The Party would seem to have effective control over *Komsomol* —or at least its Congress—but nevertheless it is concerned about the decline in the youth organization's role as a party training ground. *Komsomol* members have become less interested in, or less qualified for, party membership: while 355,174 joined the CPSU in 1962, only 312,175 joined from the larger *Komsomol* of 1965. On the opposite side of the coin, too few younger party and government functionaries are interested in *Komsomol:* only about a quarter of the deputies under thirty to the Supreme Soviet and First Secretary Leonid Brezhnev complained at the Twenty-third

[11] *KP,* April 1, 1967.
[12] *KP,* April 18, 1962.

the republican and local Soviets are *Komsomol* members.[13] CPSU Party Congress: "One cannot admit as correct a state of affairs in which only about 270,000 Communists, out of 2.5 million under thirty years of age, are working in the *Komsomol*." To draw more capable and ambitious young people into *Komsomol* work, and to increase *Komsomol's* prestige, the CPSU decided to accept people from eighteen to twenty-three into the Party only through *Komsomol*. Brezhnev also declared that party organizations "must improve their guidance of the *Komsomol*" and that it was necessary "to reinforce the Party nucleus" and "strengthen the degree of organization and discipline in the *Komsomol*." *Komsomol*, the final CPSU Congress resolution declared, "must play a bigger part in economic and cultural development."

Not only has the Party been trying to broaden the base of its leadership in *Komsomol*, but *Komsomol* is trying to improve the leaders they have. There is definitely room for improvement. Up to two-thirds of the secretaries in primary *Komsomol* units in Estonia, for example, leave annually, and many have an "everybody has only one head" to lose attitude that inhibits their effectiveness.[14] Pavlov told the Congress that on the average, regional secretaries stay on no more than two years; district secretaries last less than a year and a half, and primary secretaries about seven months. To help deal with the problem the Congress reversed an earlier statutory requirement and now allows its leaders to remain at their posts longer and develop their administrative abilities. Perhaps the most significant rural *Komsomol* program will be in the leadership area: Pavlov indicated that training courses for new primary secretaries will be started and that town organizations will be instructed to help rural ones.

*Komsomol* also is in difficult straits with its leadership of the Pioneers. Very few of the Pioneer leaders are males (only three percent in the Russian city of Ryazan, according to one survey [15]); they are in general poorly trained, and there is tremendous turnover. *Komsomolites* are notoriously reluctant to take on Pioneer work; they are selected "on the principle of whoever of the *Kom-*

---

[13] *Moscow News*, May 21, 1966.
[14] *Kommunist Estonii*, No. 12, December, 1966; *Izvestia*, March 18, 1967.
[15] *Pravda*, May 10, 1966.

*somolites* has more free time, whoever is not studying anywhere or does not have a social commission." [16]

For the time being at least the *Komsomol* leadership does not seem to have control over youth, or even much contact with it despite the Party's increasing concern with this half of the population. The youth organization has perpetuated one of the Soviet Union's most conservative programs at a time when the country seems to be attaining increasing personal freedom and prosperity. The Congress's attacks on the most popular and liberal youth magazine, *Yunost,* and on liberal trends in the arts are dramatic proof of this.[17] This, combined with a certain apathy and "formalism" among *Komsomol* leaders, has debilitated sections of the youth program that might really have attracted broad sectors of Soviet young people. A case in point is the history of the youth cafés, which were initiated in 1961 to offer young Soviets refreshments and entertainment, and thus provide an alternative to the streets and the criminal activity bred there. The cafés were originally managed jointly by *Komsomol* and the Ministry of Trade, but *Komsomol* officials gradually grew indifferent and ceded their responsibilities—mostly planning the cultural programs—to the Ministry of Trade. This was the death knell for the youth cafés as the Trade administrators were primarily concerned with meeting the plan—i.e., making a profit—and not with youth. Sales of beer and wine were stressed; whole cafés were rented out to adult groups and youths were again out in the streets. *Komsomol* also abdicated its authority over those cafés that still catered to youth. An article on sex crimes in Moscow noted that cafés and clubs had actually become the "main assembly point" of unsavory young men and "girls who can drink as hard as a man and who turn dances into indecent displays." [18] Finally, in September, 1966, the cafés were put back under joint *Komsomol*-Ministry of Trade administration with definite orders that *Komsomol* should not again relinquish its responsibilities.

[16] *KP,* February 20, 1967.

[17] For a full account of the more dramatic—though not massive—youth protests for freer artistic expression and philosophical leeway, see Michel Slavinsky, "Les jeunes intellectuels Soviétiques en lutte pour la liberté d'expression," *Est et Ouest,* 16-31 Mars 1967.

[18] *Literaturnaya Gazeta,* Moscow, July 2, 1966.

While *Komsomol* has avoided its relationship to café youth, it has directly opposed the desire of youth to flee the countryside. Attempts to leave rural areas are understandable—not only is life there dull, but earnings are lower and chances for education are more limited than in the cities. A survey in the Smolensk *oblast* showed that the number of *Komsomol* members working on state farms had halved in five years—from 12,770 to 6,256; the drop had been more precipitous at collective farms—from 21,043 to 3,780. The flight of youths in general was so bad that one *Komsomol* official declared that if "the decline in state farm youth continues at this rate, within five years we will have nobody left to work the state farms." There were villages, a party official added, "where for years no child's voice has been heard." *Literaturnaya Gazeta* [19] which published the survey, did not consider this an isolated phenomenon. It was "a powerful, objective process"—farmers have become disgruntled at lack of government attention and have gone to industrial centers for factory jobs; for youths migration has become a habit, and those parents who have not moved have urged their children to seek their livelihood elsewhere.

*Literaturnaya Gazeta* observed that the campaigns to develop areas like Siberia and Kazakhstan "had led to diminishing state interest in the non-black earth region," and the paper's warning on the flight from the countryside was that "neither enthusiasm alone, nor 'cultural living conditions' either will halt it." *Komsomol* Congress delegates, who could have drawn similar conclusions from any number of articles on the subject in preceding years, approved a final resolution calling for more development projects in Siberia, the North and the Far East, various honorary titles, medals and awards, and, finally, for *Komsomol* groups "to tackle with still greater energy" the tasks of developing farms and "cultural and educational work in the countryside." Training programs for rural *Komsomol* leaders—mentioned above—will probably get lost in the shuffle of these grandiloquent projects.

In fact, neither rural "cultural work" nor the many other similar programs the Congress ratified will get far until *Komsomol* can strengthen its administrative structure and subsequently repair its

[19] *Literaturnaya Gazeta,* July 23 and 26, 1966.

frayed ties with youth. The exchange of *Komsomol* membership cards—by reactivating the rank and file and reasserting *Komsomol's* control over them—was seen as a major way of strengthening *Komsomol* administration. But it was evident soon after the checkup began on the first day of 1967 that its goals were self-contradictory inasmuch as dilatory members were not supposed to be dropped from the organization. Somehow the *Komsomol* leaders were miraculously to turn *Komsomol* into an organization of twenty-three million enthused activists. Each member's page for "social commissions" on his new *Komsomol* card was to be filled with descriptions of work done, and harsh words in the new statute, promising expulsion for those who "compromise the high title of *Komsomol* member," seemed designed to enforce activism by the strictest means. But when some local *Komsomol* organizations in Yakutsk purged nearly 200 members within a few days for various sins of omission, they were promptly reprimanded by a higher *Komsomol* committee—and the incident was duly publicized on the front page of *Komsomolskaya Pravada* where all the other local *Komsomol* leaders would be sure to see it.[20] It was already quite plain before the year was a quarter over, and the checkup was claimed to be over half finished, that *Komsomol* just does not have twenty-three million activists. Checking up on the checkup, a *Komsomolskaya Pravda* reporter indicated that "gradually the relation between *Komsomol* activists and rank and file *Komsomolites* is starting to get back in its old rut." Any "temporary rise" in activism, he continued, "is explained only by the fact that many people were afraid that suddenly they would not be allowed to exchange" their documents.[21]

The Party's response has not been much more helpful than that of Soviet youth. In general, it has shown itself quick to blame the organization for shortcomings, but slow to entrust it with the extra authority and responsibility that might enable *Komsomol* to reactivate itself. New measures seem to play down *Komsomol's* role— perhaps to give the organization a chance to straighten itself out, perhaps from a fear that it will fail. Many sociological studies of

[20] *KP*, March 7, 1967.
[21] *KP*, March 29, 1967.

youth are now being made to help the Soviet leaders to learn more about their younger generation, but most of these studies appear to be beyond *Komsomol* control.

The reform of secondary education that was announced in November, 1966, provided for earlier specialization, optional courses, increased scientific training and improved ideological education. *Komsomol* was criticized for its work with Pioneer organizations in the schools and was told, along with party and trade union organizations, to take a greater interest in the way schoolchildren worked at home. At the Fifteenth Congress Pavlov also criticized *Komsomol,* as well as teachers, for their inactivity, which he blamed for the fact that 100,000 secondary school students are forced to repeat a grade yearly. A new post—Deputy Director of Educational Work—was created to oversee out of school work. Henceforth, *Komsomol* will have to clear its work with schoolchildren through this administrator.

The September, 1966, reform of a higher and specialized secondary education promised greater autonomy and democratization for schools. It also indicated the possibility of greater student participation in the administration of higher schools, but when this was elaborated by the Russian Republic's Minister of Higher and Specialized Secondary Education, it became clear that the areas of sports and dormitory life, as well as a greater voice in the awarding of scholarships, were the limits of "self-government." Students would continue to be represented by *Komsomol,* and *Komsomol* would continue to be subordinate to school rectors. Self-government, the minister declared, "is not a goal, but a means to attain the goal. . . . It will be an additional lever in improving the quality of training specialists."

At the Congress Pavlov had complained that "over half the postgraduate students do not present their theses on time." Rather characteristically he blamed poor organization. But to solve the problem he did not call on *Komsomol* units. He urged the Presidium of the Academy of Sciences "to give special thought" to thesis problems.

Because the Soviet government in 1964 shortened the full secondary school system by one year, from eleven to ten, two classes graduated simultaneously in 1966. Added to this double graduation was the large crop of youngsters—over four million—who left the school system after the eighth year to seek employment. The task of finding jobs and places in schools for all these youths was dubbed *Komsomol's* "shock work." *Komsomol* was left somewhat to the side, however, in the government's plan for solving the problem, which included expanding educational facilities and on-the-job training opportunities, and creating "commissions for youth employment." *Komsomol* was entrusted primarily with propagandizing the benefits of agricultural work. The accomplishments and prospects of *Komsomol's* "shock work" were hardly mentioned at the Congress.

When the anti-crime decrees were publicized in July, 1966, *Komsomol* was criticized for its performance vis-à-vis hooliganism. Yet in describing these decrees, K. I. Nikitin, a high party official, made it quite clear that *Komsomol's* only role in fighting crime would henceforth be in relation to directing young people to constructive jobs in the economy and organizing leisure time activity.[22] And there will shortly be more leisure time as the Soviet Union moves on to a five-day workweek.

The government is also faced with labor problems, especially in relation to training and mental attitude. Nearly sixty-five percent of the "rolling stones" or job transients in Moscow are under thirty; the average time between jobs in Moscow is seventeen days and in Leningrad is over twenty days.[23] Drifting workers and labor distribution are significant Soviet problems, but *Komsomol* has repeatedly been shown that regulating dormitory life is one of its main industrial functions, and it has not even been notably successful in this. At industrial enterprises many *Komsomol* organizations are obstructed by trade union and plant leaders. This is understandable because *Komsomol* is supposed to safeguard the rights of young workers (shorter hours, lighter work, special health and safety standards), a task which, if implemented, tends to disrupt the plant's operation, impede production and detract from the authority of the plant managers and trade union leaders. Many *Komsomol* leaders just give in to pressure from the plant's administrators. Many are indifferent and "reconcile themselves with the

[22] *Sovetskoye Gosudarstvo i Pravo*, November, 1966.
[23] *KP*, February 2, 1967.

facts of truancy, latenesses and bad workmanship from young workers and specialists." [24] A December, 1966, CPSU resolution criticizes *Komsomol,* and other organizations, for indifference toward working youth and instructs them to step up their performance. But the plants are far from Moscow and apparently it is typical practice to bypass the *Komsomol* organization almost completely. Recommending the experience of his party organization in the wake of a CPSU Central Committee resolution on its labor program the Party Secretary of Tula province first noted that violators of discipline were "mainly" young workers. He then gave what was evidently the party-approved cure: older workers advised novices, a council to work with teenagers was set up by the Party, the trade union or workers' group took over in the case of labor violations. *Komsomol?* Along with the personnel department it was given the job of familiarizing new workers with the plant's "history and traditions and its best people." [25]

It is not yet quite clear how much power *Komsomol* has as "overseer" of the militarization campaign. The campaign is definitely a "youth" campaign involving numerous ideological devices: rallies, research on war heroes, "open door days" at military bases, military clubs, meetings with soldiers and veterans. All these fall into the "education" phase of the campaign. Those activities that come under the heading of "training"—and which have become especially intensive in areas near China—seem to be under army control or that of DOSAAF, the Volunteer Society for Cooperation with the Army, Air Force and Navy. This part of the campaign includes a training flotilla for boys from twelve to seventeen, military games for schoolchildren and "military-patriotic schools" to teach youngsters skills such as those of artillerymen, border guards and radio operators. Those are the kind of jobs that soldiers can do best, and it appears that the army has essential control over the training aspects of the program, despite the fact that *Komsomol* is strongly represented in the army. Whatever role *Komsomol* plays in the ideological side of the program it must share with DOSAAF and the army.

One of the gravest blows to the *Komsomol* ego may have come

[24] *KP,* December 24, 1966.
[25] *Pravda,* April 8, 1967.

in the Pioneer program, which has long been *Komsomol's* special responsibility. For months before the *Komsomol* Central Committee met to discuss the program, articles had appeared in *Komsomolskaya Pravda* concerning the values and shortcomings of organizing Pioneer units outside of schools. The articles called for setting them up not only where the children live but also on the basis of special interests which would make them more enthusiastic about the program. Such out of school units would have given *Komsomol* greater responsibility inasmuch as the school units come under the jurisdiction of teachers, who more often than not do not belong to *Komsomol*. However, the Central Committee refused to ratify the idea. Conceding that out of school units "enjoy enormous popularity among the youngsters," Pavlov declared that the class Pioneer detachment would remain "the chief group to which the Pioneer bears responsibility. . . ." Any other Pioneer groups are to be subordinate to the school-centered groups. Revealing that *Komsomol* often had too little to do with the Pioneers, Pavlov also attacked the councils that oversee the Pioneers. Although *Komsomol* is the official guardian of the Pioneers, Pavlov noted that province councils were often "inordinately large," and set up on the principle of "let us not overlook anyone"; nevertheless, this did not prevent them from forgetting to put the district and city *Komsomol* first secretaries on the council. To help them solve Pioneer problems *Komsomol* has suggested setting up "a research institution on the theory and methodology of the Pioneer movement."

These examples are all part of the trend for the *Komsomol* to call in outside help when faced with a tough youth problem. Increasingly other government and party organizations work directly with youth—in schools or factories or on the street—rather than entrust the job directly to *Komsomol*. *Komsomol* of course has contributed to the situation by the apathy, bureaucracy and careerism of its administrators, which has further widened the gap between *Komsomol* and youth. Meanwhile, the Party has contributed to the breach by giving some encouragement to "liberalization": in the economic reforms, increased educational decentralization, new ideas of legal practice, talk of "student self-government," limited ideological thaw, greater emphasis on consumer goods.

While it may not be overloading *Komsomol* with new commissions, the Party has not abandoned the youth organization either. *Komsomol's* ideological program is still as broad as it is utopian, and the youth league is still expected to recruit large numbers of workers for special projects in the North and Far East.

But the Party has expressed serious criticism of *Komsomol,* and it has instigated measures to extend party tutelage and improve *Komsomol* administration. It hopes that these steps will make *Komsomol* more attractive and effective.

Nevertheless, the main problem does not seem to have been faced. Among the primary reasons youth has become less interested in *Komsomol* is that they consider the organization dull, old-fashioned and conservative; and no doubt they consider themselves truer to revolutionary ideals than *Komsomol.* For although *Komsomol* pays lip service to "revolutionary, labor and fighting traditions," its official newspaper contradicts these traditions in front page editorials:

> We do not ask: *do you want* to become an economist? We suggest that you consider: *are you ready* consciously to select the most necessary, most important and completely poetic—we underline that!—profession? Are you ready to become a Soviet businessman? A financier? [26]

The Party's inclination in the past has been to treat youth more strictly than other sectors of the population just because it is young and by nature more rebellious. It is possible, however, that continuing, if not increasing, signs of youthful alienation may convince the Party to take a daring new step—to woo youth with a more liberal program: elements of real self-government, less ideology and more responsibility. The risks of encouraging too much "anarchy" might be rewarded with the increased activity and dedication of the generation that is about to take the reins of Soviet power.

[26] *KP,* February 19, 1967.

# 5

## Recent Changes in Soviet Educational Policy

NICHOLAS DeWITT

THIS CHAPTER should perhaps be subtitled, "The Silent Death of Khrushchev's School Reforms." As is well-known, Soviet education has received a great deal of publicity in the world press in the last ten years. The American press has not been an exception, and to some the talk about the problems of education in Russia is commonplace. Yet when the question is asked as to what subject is really the most important in studying educational development around the world it becomes apparent that the answer is to be found in the basic models of society and the education which serves them—the pluralistic model and the monistic model. Among the former, the United States is a prime example. Among the latter, the Soviet model of Communist education is unique. Without an understanding of what the Russians have been trying to do over the last five decades in their attempt to reshape the human intellect through education, the meaning of many national liberation and national development models cannot be readily studied.

In short, over the last few years in many developing nations there has been an almost impulsive desire to look at the Soviet development model and particularly its educational effort as a

Nicholas DeWitt is Associate Professor in the Departments of Economics and Government at Indiana University and Director of the International Survey of Educational Development and Planning.

blueprint for remaking their societies in a hurry. The education of
the "new Soviet man" hangs invariably as a mirage—tempting,
and to be followed. In the meantime Soviet education has been in a
state of enormous turmoil for no reason other than the very inade-
quacy of performance of such a model over the long run. The
history of Soviet educational development and planning serves as a
perfect example of the inefficiency and ineffectiveness of short-
term "solutions" for long-range problems. The reforms and
changes over the last fifty years might be used to illustrate this
point, but it has become particularly apparent in the last ten years.

First, it must be recognized that Soviet school reforms are attempts to change the school system from above so as to make it
more responsive to pressing national needs. The basic assumption
is that the State, the national government and its arm, the central
planning board, knows and can predict the basis for determining
what kind of and how much education individuals ought to have.
In the Soviet Union, as anywhere else, the "demand" for education
is largely a reflection of the continuous rise of educational aspirations of parents for their children. These private aspirations are
fostered further by the regime's system of motivations and incentives, which bestows monetary rewards and prestige upon a highly
educated elite.

However, these educational aspirations of parents and youth
represent only potential demand, or what Soviet authorities often
call "subjective demand." On top of this potential demand, the
state planning body, *Gosplan,* superimposes upon all educational
institutions, and particularly on upper secondary and higher education, a somewhat different "demand function." It is claimed that it
is an "objective" derived demand, which establishes actual needs
and requirements which can be estimated through a complex
method of nationwide projections for personnel with a given occupational skill and the derived educational specialization.

The three major pillars of the Soviet system of national and
centralized planning are termed "balances." They are material, or
allocation of commodity flows; financial, or allocation of monetary
flows; and labor, or allocation of human resource flows. In essence
the labor balance consists of a checkerboard method of ascertain-
ing for each occupation and industry sector, where people are

presently employed, and where new additions to the present stock can be obtained, and with which specific qualifications, that is, education, training and experience.

In essence, the source of supply in that labor balance constitutes detailed tabulations by occupation, education and place of future employment of the new accessions to the labor force. The majority of these new accessions are youths aged fifteen to twenty. Their assimilation into the labor force simply means the termination of their formal education. This in turn means that all educational institutions on the secondary school level and beyond are given annual admission quotas. Each educational establishment determines how to fill its respective quota in order to assure the proper "output" several years thereafter. Soviet educational institutions select their own students on the basis of merit, both academic and political, and in accordance with a national and uniform set of rules and requirements. Each institution trains its students in accordance with nationally prescribed curricula and syllabi. The training task completed, each institution gets its annual "placement schedule" for the graduating class of that year.

Every Soviet textbook on manpower and economic planning asserts that the two techniques, namely the "staff method" and the "coefficient method," used for estimating these quotas for the output of graduates are an efficient means of planning education. In reality, however, as Khrushchev himself declared in 1959:

> We do not have any scientifically reliable method of estimating how many and what kind of specialists we need in different branches of the national economy, what the future demand will be for a certain kind of specialist, and when such a demand will arise.[1]

And as Soviet authorities acknowledge:

> The planning organs still do not have at the present time the scientifically founded methodology for estimating the demand for specialists either for the national economy as a whole or for its individual branches. There is no methodology which allows us to take into consideration the most significant factors which influence increases or decreases in the demand for specialists in relationship

[1] *Pravda,* July 2, 1959.

to the further growth of socialist production and the development of science, culture and technical progress.[2]

The message is loud and clear, but many turn a deaf ear to it. All who are involved in manpower and educational planning missions in developing nations should take cognizance of Soviet experience. The translation of occupational and employment targets into demand for educational output is at best an uncertain art.

These admissions are pertinent to the current turmoil in Soviet education and particularly to the interpretation of "polytechnical education" in the context of the current reforms. The debate on the content of "polytechnical instruction" in relation to general education and academic subjects continues to rage in the Soviet pedagogical press. All ideological verbalisms about "polytechnism" aside, the Soviet authorities over the last decade have been searching for the meaning of "polytechnism" in pragmatic, operational terms: how to prepare people for work and how to keep them working. It is in this context that ever since the inception of Khrushchev's educational reform in 1958, dark clouds of controversy have never left the Soviet educational arena.

For almost three decades prior to 1958 the Soviet system of education had a rather stable structure. It operated a system of primary, junior secondary and senior secondary schools with a grade structure of 4-3-3. By design, this Stalinist educational system was geared to the development of a "learned elite," persons who, having devoted themselves almost exclusively to higher specialized learning, never worked with their hands. To be sure, social ethos and Marxist disquisitions demanded that their academic studies be related to "production" and to "labor," but neither of these was adequately defined. So long as the number of highly educated persons was relatively small and so long as they could be provided with white-collar and supervisory jobs, the emphasis on training a technocratic elite caused little problem. But as the output of the Soviet educational system increased by leaps and

[2] G. S. Anodin, *Opredelenie potrebnosti v spetsialistakh v promyshlennosti: iz opyta ugol'noi promyshlennosti* (Determination of Demand for Specialists in Industry: On the Basis of Experience in the Coal Industry), Moscow, 1959, pp. 6-7.

bounds, it no longer became possible to give white-collar and supervisory jobs to all specialists. This heralded the beginning of reforms in education which resulted, on the one hand, in the diversion of students into applied training on the secondary level and, on the other, in the expansion of part-time evening and extension-correspondence programs combining practical work with study.

In the nineteen-fifties secondary schooling was expanding more rapidly than other components of the educational system. This rapid expansion of secondary schooling was responsible in part for the educational reforms, the adjustment of the academic curriculum to the needs of *diversified* and vocationally oriented training. In the late nineteen-fifties, first through a process of piecemeal adjustment and then by radical institutional reform, primary-secondary schools became institutions for turning out students who, in addition to having academic preparation, were trained in labor skills and thus ready for employment. The 1958 reforms changed the school grade structure to a 4-4-3 system, with the addition of mandatory vocational training in the three upper grades of secondary school. The meaning of these educational reforms, because of their complexity, was at least a controversial one not only among Western students of Soviet society but among the Soviet planners, educationalists and parents. In the early nineteen-sixties as the reform progressed, most of the official Soviet press was singing praises of its successful fulfillment by 1965. Occasionally, however, highly skeptical voices were heard about its purpose and effectiveness.

Just as the deadline of its full implementation was approaching in the summer of 1964, the Soviet government abruptly decreed the elimination of certain major features of Khrushchev's educational program. The timing of the reform and some of its features were measures designed to speed up additions to the Soviet labor force of young people with skill qualifications who were needed to alleviate the shortages caused by demographic trends. The sharp drop in the birthrate caused by wartime losses affected the Soviet school age population throughout the nineteen-fifties and curtailed the availability of new entrants to the work force in the early nineteen-sixties. The reform was aimed at alleviating this situation;

and as the emergency eased, the reform lost its meaning, and some of its labor-channeling features were scrapped by the Soviet government in 1964.

In August, 1964, the Central Committee of the Communist party and the Council of Ministers of the Soviet Union decreed a cutback from eleven years of primary-secondary school to ten years, the length it had been before the reform. The Minister of Education of the Russian Soviet Federated Socialist Republic declared that the "prolongation of secondary schooling by one year, which was devoted largely to production training, has not justified itself in most cases." He added that production training as currently implemented was "frequently a useless waste of time," and "was creating serious opposition on the part of students, their parents and society." The 1964 change transformed schools to a 4-4-2 grade structure, eliminating vocational training and part-time employment in the upper secondary schools.[3]

This shift was not entirely surprising for in earlier studies it was argued that the major aim of Khrushchev's school reform was based on short-run considerations. The solution of superimposing on the standard general education curriculum a localized system of supplemental labor training shaped in accordance with local economic needs and the availability of skilled training outlets did not produce the desired results. First, students who received specific vocational skill training did not in many cases enter employment in the same skill. Meanwhile, the reform's emphasis on vocational-technical training in the general education schools and part-time employment of upper secondary school students resulted in a considerable deterioration of standards and quality of instruction. This had an adverse effect not only in primary-secondary general education, but also in semi-professional and professional training programs, which were forced to absorb graduates of general education schools who now had worse preparation than before. Finally, the separate network of Soviet vocational-technical schools, which is specifically geared to apprenticeship training in economic enterprises, was handicapped in recruiting students.

[3] For the detailed discussion see: E. I. Afanasenko, "Zadachi Sovetskoi Shkoly" (Tasks of Soviet Schools), in *Uchitel'skaya Gazeta* (Teachers Gazette), August 13, 1964.

Since Khrushchev's brand of "polytechnism" did not work, in the summer of 1964 the government of the Soviet Union created a mammoth commission on curricular contents for primary and secondary education. It is still at work, and its recommendations have not yet been reported. But if and when they are, they will be implemented by an entirely new administrative setup.

For several decades the Soviet Union had the pretense of having a decentralized system of primary-secondary education. Under this setup various union and autonomous national republics had their own separate ministries of education. The Russian Soviet Federated Socialist Republic (RSFSR) had in a sense primacy, and, with its research arm, the Academy of Pedagogical Sciences, set the pace for curricular content and teaching practices in the entire Soviet Union. Through its Administration on Instruction and Methodology (*Uchebno-Metodicheskoe Upravlenie*) and the Russian SFSR Academy of Pedagogical Sciences (*Akademiia Pedagogicheskikh Nauk RSFSR*), the Russian SFSR Ministry of Education played a key role in formulating model standards in regard to such matters as school curricula, textbooks, teaching methods and examinations. The Russian SFSR Academy of Pedagogical Sciences is also the major curricular research center of the Soviet Union. Several ministries of education in other Union republics have pedagogical research institutes, which adapt centrally prescribed programs of instruction to local conditions, primarily adjusting programs to the linguistic and/or geographic peculiarities of a given republic. The ministries of education of the remaining republics followed the pattern of the Russian SFSR Ministry of Education, making only minor modifications to suit local conditions.

This is all past history now. In August, 1966, the Supreme Soviet of the Soviet Union modified the Soviet Constitution and decreed the establishment of an all-Union Ministry of Public Education, which is to develop a unified and standard system of primary-secondary education for the entire country. Among other things, this new central Ministry of Education is to see that the speedy "eradication" of the "past educational policies and practices," namely Khrushchev's reform measures, is to be undertaken. The new ministry will be in charge of all phases of the long-range planning of education, including not only the contents of general education but polytechnical and labor vocational training as well.[4] It will determine not only what is to be taught, but how many ought to be taught.

There are two components in the Soviet educational system which must be clearly distinguished. First, the general education schools discussed above, which until the mid-nineteen-fifties were primarily concerned with the preparation of students for higher education, offered an academic curriculum and are now being reformed into some sort of "multipurpose" schools. The second component consisted of a system of schools specifically aimed at training semiskilled and skilled manpower and, on the secondary level, semiprofessionals. This division of functions reflects the philosophy of Soviet education, which stipulates that specialized education could be offered more efficiently in a *separate* system of school facilities. Semiprofessional schools have been providing for the necessary diversity in training which the standard curriculum, one-track, academic secondary schools did not. In the last three years the training functions of the semiprofessional schools were strengthened and their enrollments considerably expanded. In addition, students who formerly terminated general education at eight-year schools will be absorbed into the lower level vocational-technical schools, the network of which has also been greatly expanded for the training of skilled workers. In the last three years there has also been a considerable shift in priorities for specialized secondary education.

In the summer of 1963 the Council of Ministers of the Soviet Union reviewed the status of specialized manpower training and decreed one very significant measure. It stipulated that the tempo of secondary semiprofessional education should be speeded up over that of higher education. This was a new departure. The Soviet planners decreed a radically new target for the output of semiprofessional graduates. They stipulated that the Soviet economy should have a ratio of three or four semiprofessional to one professional graduate. They claimed that objective factors, new technology and new organization of economic activity, were responsible for the shift in these ratios, from the present ratio of about three semiprofessionals to two professionals.

---

[4] *Uchitel'skaya Gazeta,* August 6, 1966, and September 10, 1966.

This means that if the present recommendations are carried out, the output of graduates from semiprofessional schools—and thus enrollments—should be about two to two and one-half times greater than in higher education, while at the present time total semiprofessional enrollments (about 3,300,00) are still lower than those in higher education (3,600,000). The reason for this shift in policy is obvious: semiprofessional admissions would go over 1,000,000 per year, which would siphon off some of the applicants pressing now for admission to higher education.

Post-secondary school training in the Soviet Union is carried out in a system of institutions of higher education. In many respects Soviet higher education is different from that in America and most West European countries. All higher education in the Soviet Union is public, and all higher education programs are designed to develop individual talent for specialized professional employment. In addition, all Soviet higher educational establishments are professionally oriented. The Soviet Union does not have any general education or liberal arts colleges or nonprofessionally oriented undergraduate programs of instruction such as are commonly found in American colleges and universities. Soviet institutions of higher learning combine under one roof undergraduate college education and the professional school training of American universities: Soviet students trained in these various types of universities or institutes follow standardized curricula and receive diplomas (but not degrees) upon graduation. The Soviet philosophy of higher education is firmly rooted in the conviction that man is destined to perform a specific task in society. Those who advance into higher education, therefore, must become specialists so that they may make maximum use of their capabilities. What makes Soviet higher education a distinct development in the concept of functional education is the *degree* of specialization derived from formal training.

The student's field of study in higher education is designated by the term "specialty" (*spetsial'nost'*). All students acquire a specialty as a result of higher education study. This applies to any field of knowledge, be it science, engineering, literature, the fine arts, ballet, school teaching or medicine. The Soviet student chooses his specialty at the time he enters higher education, then embarks on a well defined program which he must complete in order to qualify as a "specialist" in the narrow occupational meaning of the term. "Specialization" in the Soviet Union, therefore, has considerably narrower meaning than in American professional education. It entails training in an individual, narrowly defined field of professional knowledge, which will equip the student to perform a given occupational job.

The piecemeal undoing of certain provisions of Khrushchev's educational reform really began with higher and secondary specialized education. On May 21, 1964, as Khrushchev was traveling in Egypt, the Central Committee of the Communist Party of the Soviet Union and the Council of Ministers of the Soviet Union adopted a decree concerning the "further improvement" of specialized education. It ordered the curtailment of the length of training in higher education and secondary specialized schools by anywhere from six to eighteen months, thus restoring the pre-reform length of training in higher education from four to five and one-half years, depending upon specialty, and in the secondary specialized schools to three to four years. Thus, in 1964-65 all types of specialized training establishments began to follow the path set for pedagogical training, which was cut from five to four years in May of 1963.

The reason given for this wholesale conversion was that the year to year and one-half devoted to practical experience was "no longer necessary," for the majority of those entering those educational institutions either had had two or more years of employment experience or else had already acquired a working specialty while in secondary school.

The Ministry of Higher and Secondary Specialized Education was given the right to arrange the "most rational time for industrial practice and work experience of the students over the entire length of their study, concentrating both, however, at upper courses." The ministry was also ordered to curtail some of the narrow specialties which had been established in the preceding five years. In view of the cut in the length of study, the ministry further decreed a complete review of all curricula and syllabi in specialized fields in order to eliminate the duplication of instructional material and in order to transfer not "absolutely essential courses" from the category of "required" to "optional overload electives." The motto now is "Save and make the most efficient use of the student's time." Since industrial practice and work experience are to be concentrated in the upper courses, present indications are that these curricular revisions will improve basic preparation of students in the first three years and will free students from the "drudgery of labor" in the first few years of study. This is an obvious undoing of Khrushchev's work and study plan. In September, 1966, the Soviet government introduced another set of sweeping measures aimed at improving the quality of university education. The universities were granted more freedom in academic, administrative and—most important—research activities in order to improve the quality of higher education.

Another major development concerns extension-correspondence and evening education. Part-time higher and secondary specialized education, though introduced in the late nineteen-thirties, is really a post-war development in the Soviet Union. It gained particular impetus from Khrushchev's school reforms. "Study while you work," was his slogan. In April, 1964, the Central Committee of the Communist Party and the Council of Ministers of the Soviet Union decreed the further expansion of evening and extension-correspondence education and called particularly for its qualitative improvement. It is the latter which causes the major headache for Soviet planners. While the success rate of students in day programs is seventy-five to eighty percent, in part-time programs less than one out of five entering students completes five or six years of study. Although the quality of part-time specialized education remains poor in comparison with daytime instruction programs, its quantitative gains, particularly under Khrushchev's prodding, have been spectacular. Admissions and enrollments in part-time programs have multiplied five times in the last ten years and have now outstripped day programs by a substantial margin. By the fall of 1966 two-thirds of all students in Soviet higher and secondary specialized schools were in evening and extension-correspondence programs.

This enormous expansion of part-time education was due to a variety of factors. First, it was considered convenient and cheap, for it did not require additional capital outlays for instructional and residential facilities. It permitted more intensive utilization of existing staffs. And above all, it used the student's leisure time without withdrawing him from his current employment position in the economy. But all of these considerations apparently were not enough to give it a clear advantage. The quality of training was abysmally bad. Despite impressive "numbers" the efficiency was very low. Above all the primary purpose of part-time education was usurped: persons who allegedly trained in part-time programs to improve their current occupational proficiency were actually retraining themselves for another and totally unrelated occupation. For these reasons action was taken in September, 1966. The Council of Ministers of the Soviet Union and the Central Committee of the Communist Party decreed that "as the practical experience of the past years has demonstrated that the training of specialists in day programs has indisputable superiority not only as far as quality of education is concerned, but also in terms of lesser economic wastefulness," for most professional occupations, future expansion of higher education should proceed in day divisions. Only selected specialties should be left to part-time education and all major types of professional occupations should be trained in higher education on a full-time basis. New "sandwich" programs are to be encouraged, but on the job experience and industrial practice are to be postponed to the last two years of study.

This essay has highlighted only some of the major developments in the piecemeal undoing of Khrushchev's educational reform. Leaving some of the details aside, what is the major problem?

Soviet educational policy has been for decades in the past, and will continue for decades in the future, to be confronted by two interacting forces. The first is the role education must play as a weapon in the hands of the Communist dictatorship in the social, political and, particularly, the economic transformation of Soviet society. The second is the end product of that education: the Soviet citizen as an individual, his self-growth and the development of his knowledge, intellect and skill and his desire for education of his own choosing. Over the last two decades the Soviet planners have intensified their drive to implant, through formal education as much as possible and as early as possible, some kind of basic functional skill or specialty which would enable the State to integrate the individual into productive employment and which would help to retain him in that employment. This policy continues. Either for self-enlightenment or for personal gain, the individual seeks out educational opportunities which will, at least in the formal sense, advance his status in Soviet society. Fundamentally, the individual is seeking out what he can get from the State by partaking of as much education as possible at the least cost to himself.

My thesis is that only by looking at these two problems in their interaction may we find clues to recent changes in Soviet educational policies and practices. The Soviet individual and the Soviet State are engaged in a highly pragmatic game: who gets what out of whom. I feel that most of the ideological disquisitions and verbal exercises with scriptural utterings of Marxism-Leninism have little bearing upon the actual practices of developing trained manpower potential for the Soviet Union. Stalin denounced the pre-revolutionary past; Khrushchev denounced Stalin's epoch, and now Khrushchev's heirs denounce his era by relying upon the same passages from the Marxist-Leninist scriptures about what an ideal education should accomplish in training the ideal individual for the ideal Communist society. The study of theory and philosophy of Soviet education gives very little clue to action and practical solutions. Essentially, the problems of Soviet education are not significantly different from those anywhere else. As society gets more complex the short-term expediencies and monistic solutions simply must give way to greater pluralism in arriving at a long-run equilibrium. Basically, the Soviet citizen asks himself, "What's an education good for anyway?" The Soviet State is asking the same question.

# 6

## Philosophy: A New Openness

JAMES P. SCANLAN

AT A CONFERENCE in Moscow not long ago a prominent Soviet philosopher told his colleagues that only two beliefs are obligatory for Marxist philosophers: that matter is primary, and that the world is knowable. Beyond these basic dogmas, he asserted, everything is open to discussion. The observation evidently met with general approval; it was repeated to this author by other Soviet philosophers with a satisfaction approaching pride.

Openness to discussion has not been a conspicuous feature of Soviet philosophy since the nineteen-twenties. The Bolshevik revolution brought Russia an official philosophy: the dialectical materialism of Karl Marx and Friedrich Engels, as developed and interpreted by Vladimir Lenin. Despite the fact that this philosophy was from the beginning conceived by its proponents as the only adequate map of reality and guide to political action, it had in its early years a vitality and flexibility that permitted genuine debate. But under Stalin, in the nineteen-thirties and nineteen-forties, it hardened into an orthodoxy that left little room for disagreement; indeed deviation from established doctrines came to be considered a crime. Even in the years since Stalin's death in 1953 the monolithic philosophy of dialectical materialism solidified under Stalin has continued to rule Soviet thought and the Soviet educational

James P. Scanlan is Professor of Philosophy at Goucher College in Towson, Baltimore, Maryland.

system to a degree which seems to belie the statement that only two beliefs are obligatory for Marxist philosophers.

Yet the statement cannot be ignored. It is, at least, symptomatic of a change of attitude in the post-Stalin age. Disagreement and discussion are less feared, and if they are not yet manifested dramatically in publicized debates or in the development of opposing schools in Soviet philosophy, they are expressed progressively in small changes that could have big results.

For an undergraduate philosophy student at Moscow University, for example, the changes of the past ten years already have made a significant difference. He now has a far better chance of broadening his philosophical horizons. He will, of course, still become a Marxist. But he will become a Marxist with a greater understanding of philosophical alternatives to Marxism and with a greater sense of the excitement of philosophical discussion within Marxism.

Granted, in many respects his philosophical education differs little from that of his Stalinist predecessor. He and his two thousand fellow philosophy majors at Moscow University—some seven hundred of them full-time students on campus—follow a heavy schedule of prescribed courses in science and the humanities in addition to their courses in philosophy. The required philosophy courses in his five-year undergraduate program still focus strongly on the truth of dialectical materialism and the errors of Western, "bourgeois" thinkers. The syllabus for his course in ethics still states that "Communist morality is the highest stage in the moral progress of mankind," and announces that the central principle of morality is "devotion to communism, love of the socialist Fatherland." In his five-year course in "the history of foreign philosophy" his knowledge of Plato, Aristotle and their Western successors is still drawn largely from Marxist secondary sources. He still reads that "the philosophy of Thomas Aquinas with all its absurdities was a reflection of the feudal, serf mode of life which then prevailed in Europe," and that American pragmatism is the philosophy of "vigorous money-grabbers." The reading lists for all his philosophy courses still consist almost entirely of works by Marx, Engels, Lenin and more recent Soviet writers (now excluding Stalin, of course).

The Soviet student of philosophy still finds his required lectures

—thirty to thirty-five hours a week—for the most part a dull repetition of dogma, and he works, drowses or talks with his neighbors through them—or even reads a newspaper in plain view of the lecturer. He still finds a branch office of the Communist party in the philosophy building of Moscow University. He is still expected to be an atheist, and the expectation is fortified by required courses demonstrating the untruth and the socially pernicious character of all religions. He still will not hear criticisms of Lenin as a philosopher from any podium. He still finds only "approved" books on the open shelves in the libraries, and must make special requests for other literature.

On the other hand, other literature is increasingly available. And if the Soviet student is energetic and resourceful, he will find it much more feasible than it was ten years ago to acquaint himself with the breadth of philosophical opinion both within and beyond Marxism.

Since 1956 more works by non-Soviet philosophers have been translated into Russian than in the whole preceding quarter of a century. Many, of course, are books by Western Marxists which accept more or less fully the doctrines of Soviet philosophy. Others, though in some respects they present modes of analysis or criticism which are consistent with Soviet Marxism, do provide Russian readers with much new information concerning other philosophical movements. Such are Ernest Gellner's critique of linguistic philosophy, *Words and Things* (translated in 1962), and the study of existentialist thought, *From Schopenhauer to Heidegger,* by the Swiss philosopher, Theodore Schwartz, translated in 1964. Most significant is the growing list of works representing positions to which dialectical materialism has been considered hostile. Ludwig Wittgenstein's seminal *Tractatus Logico-Philosophicus,* for example, was translated in 1958. The text is preceded by an introduction warning readers against the "unsound subjective-idealist epistemological constructions of the author," but the translation which follows is accurate and complete. Other contemporary works, similarly introduced, which have been presented to Soviet readers in recent years are Nikolai Hartmann's *Aesthetics* (translated in 1958), Norbert Wiener's *Cybernetics and Society* (1961) and Thomas E. Hill's *Contemporary Theories of Knowl-*

*edge* (1965). Bertrand Russell is represented by three titles: *Human Knowledge, Its Scope and Limits* (1957), *Why I am Not a Christian* (1958) and *History of Western Philosophy* (1959). Works in logic and the philosophy of science by Rudolf Carnap, Philip Frank, and Hans Reichenbach have also been published in translation. Wittgenstein's *Philosophical Investigations* has been translated but is not yet published. The number of these translations is still small, and they are issued in limited printings. But by comparison with earlier years they constitute a significant trend.

Philosophical classics, both Russian and Western, are also appearing in increasing numbers. Russian thinkers previously ignored or condemned as philosophically pernicious by Marxist scholars are being republished, some for the first time in the Soviet period. The works of the eighteenth century Ukrainian religious philosopher, Gregory Skovoroda, were published in two volumes in 1961. Peter Lavrov, the nineteenth century Russian Populist thinker, long condemned as a "subjective idealist," is now represented by a two-volume collection, published in 1965, in which Lavrov is introduced as a thinker "many-sided and rich" who, for all his errors, deserves "an honored place in the history of socialist thought." In 1966 a two-volume set of works by Russian deists of the eighteenth and early nineteenth centuries was published. And even more attention is being given to the classics of Western philosophy. There are new translations of Aristotle's *On the Soul* and his *Metaphysics*. New editions of Bacon's *New Atlantis* and many of Hegel's works have appeared. Leibniz's correspondence with Samuel Clarke was published in 1960. Since 1957, collections of philosophical works, many never before translated into Russian, by a considerable number of Western thinkers have become available: Herder, Goethe and Diderot in one-volume editions, Spinoza, Gassendi, Hobbes, Hume, Holbach and Locke in two volumes, Rousseau in three volumes, Immanuel Kant in six volumes. Now in press or released within the past year are Schelling's *Philosophy of Art*, Bayle's *Historical and Critical Dictionary*, a four-volume *Anthology of World Philosophy*, a three-volume anthology entitled *English Materialists of the Eighteenth Century*, a three-volume set of Plato's *Dialogues*, and a three-volume collection of Ludwig Feuerbach's works in the history of philosophy. In addition, there is a new series of biographies of classical Western thinkers: volumes on Aquinas, Epicurus, Giordano Bruno, Montesquieu, Herder and Fichte already have been published.

Of the books now available to a Russian student of philosophy, none show so clear a shift of attitude as the successive dictionaries and encyclopedias of philosophy that have been published since Stalin's death. The 1955 printing of the 1952 *Concise Philosophical Dictionary* still carried a long and glowing article on Stalin as a philosopher, with a full-page portrait. But the concluding sentence of the original article had already been deleted. It had read: "The immortal name of Joseph Stalin will live forever in the minds and hearts of the Russian people." In 1963 a new edition—shorter but called simply *Philosophical Dictionary*—omitted the immortal name altogether, except for a reference in its preface to the "enormous damage" done by "the cult of Stalin." More important, the 1963 edition is consistently less abusive, less chauvinistic, and philosophically more comprehensive and sophisticated than its Stalinist ancestors. It drops the entry "Great October Socialist Revolution," and while it still has an entry on "Patriotism," the earlier succeeding entry "Patriotism, Soviet" is gone. A good many of the separate entries for books by Lenin have been omitted. In its new articles the 1963 edition reflects a growing Soviet interest in formal logic, the philosophy of science and other areas of concern to contemporary Western philosophers. Modern mathematical logic, once rejected as incompatible with dialectical materialism, is represented by a large number of entries not included in earlier editions. Cybernetics, earlier condemned as a "bourgeois pseudo-science," is also represented by a number of new entries. And for the first time there are articles on Sartre, Husserl, Jaspers, Heidegger, Carnap, Whitehead, Wittgenstein and other twentieth century Western thinkers.

The 1963 dictionary was praised publicly in 1965 in *Voprosy filosofii* (*Problems of Philosophy*), the leading Soviet philosophical journal, for being free "in large measure" from "the dogmatic style of philosophizing." But despite its advances it was actually criticized in the same journal for not going far enough in analyzing —from a Marxist point of view, of course—the latest trends in

Western philosophy. Further movement in this direction is suggested in a new pocket *Concise Dictionary of Philosophy* published in 1966. This book, though more compact than the 1963 dictionary, has slightly longer articles on such topics in the Marxist interpretation of Western philosophy as "subjective idealism," "objective idealism," "irrationalism" and "intuitivism."

Concurrently, publication of a major, multi-volume *Philosophical Encyclopedia* was begun in the Soviet Union in 1960. To date about half the alphabet has been covered in three volumes. This work still points out dutifully the "errors" of non-Marxist thinkers, asserting, for example, that absolute idealism is based on "the false assumption of the existence of an absolute idea," and calling John Dewey "a defender of American imperialism." On the other hand much solid and accurate information is presented in the work, which is comparable in scope but far more detailed than the one-volume 1963 dictionary. Major Western philosophers are included, with extensive bibliographies of their works. And a number of Russian thinkers who fell from favor earlier in the Soviet period, such as Abram Deborin and Lyubov Aksel'rod, are included, also with bibliographies. Not all the disgraced thinkers have been rehabilitated, however; Nikolai Bukharin is still missing. But on the whole the *Encyclopedia* is a treasure-house of information previously unavailable to the Soviet reader.

In the formal course work for his major in philosophy, the Russian student will also find less abuse of Western philosophy and increased attention to non-Marxist viewpoints and genuine philosophical problems. His required four-year course in the history of Russian philosophy, for example, places heavy emphasis on those strains in Russian thought which can be considered anticipations of, or at least partially consistent with, Marxism. But other strains are not ignored, and two or three two-hour lectures may be devoted to a "reactionary" Russian religious thinker such as Vladimir Solovyov or Fëdor Dostoevski, whose views will be presented in some detail and sometimes without noticeable slanting. Here much depends upon the professor. Russian professors, like their counterparts in other countries, differ considerably in ability and degree of partisanship. The younger Russian philosophers, those who have been trained within the past ten years, seem less bound to Marxist concepts in presenting material to their students. The students have great respect for those who succeed in giving them fresh, substantial insights not available in a hundred older textbooks.

Of the philosophy courses at Moscow University greatest interest is aroused by the "special courses" (*spetskursy*) each student is required to take. In satisfying this requirement the student may choose among a number of topics currently offered by various professors. During the academic year 1964-1965 thirteen such courses were given in philosophy (besides those administered by the Philosophy Faculty but actually in psychology and social science). Their subjects were: problems in the criticism of neopositivism, critique of existentialism, critique of contemporary bourgeois philosophy of history, problems in the origin of philosophy, communism and religion, matter and consciousness, the problem of form, Marxism-Leninism's campaign against anarchism, Marxist-Leninist methodology in the history of philosophy and critique of contemporary bourgeois conceptions of the history of philosophy, logical semantics, methodological questions in the social sciences, determinism (*zakonomernost'*) and the formation of spiritual development, critique of the ideology of *Signposts* and the "God-seekers" (early twentieth century Russian religious thinkers).

As is evident from these titles, many of the special courses have contemporary Western philosophy as their subject matter. Others focus on problems prominent in contemporary Western philosophy. And though many are formally "critiques," the students nonetheless make use of contemporary materials and write papers based on readings which include Western texts. Thus a student, if he can lay his hands on the appropriate books, might read philosophical works by Jean-Paul Sartre and write a paper on some aspect of Sartre's philosophy.

The chief obstacle, of course, is still the availability of the books. Significant as the growing number of Russian translations is, it is yet only a fraction of the works required for serious study of problems in contemporary philosophy. Even if the student reads other languages, he is severely limited in his access to Western works, since the works in their original languages are very difficult to find.

The books do exist, of course, in the largest scholarly libraries. The card catalogue of the Lenin Library in Moscow, the nation's leading research library, in 1965 listed thirty-nine titles for Jean-Paul Sartre, ten for A. J. Ayer, twenty-two for Rudolf Carnap, fifty-four for Bertrand Russell, eighteen for Martin Heidegger, thirty-three for Karl Jaspers. Gilbert Ryle's *The Concept of Mind* is there, and so are J. L. Austin's *Philosophical Papers* and *Sense and Sensibilia*. But there are also some curious omissions: Wittgenstein's *Tractatus* and his *Blue and Brown Books* are listed, but not (in 1965) his *Philosophical Investigations*. The twentieth century Russian theologian, philosopher and physicist, Paul Florensky, is represented in the card catalogue by his technical and scientific works, but his theological masterpiece, *The Pillar and the Ground of Truth,* is not listed. (It is in the library's collection, however, and can be read by a qualified research scholar. The same is true of pre-revolutionary Russian theological journals, such as the *Moscow Theological Herald.* They are in the library but their presence is not advertised, even in the general card catalogue.) Bukharin, like other, still suspect figures such as Leon Trotsky, is not included in the catalogue at all.

But one library copy of an important work cannot serve the entire philosophical community of Moscow, and for many prospective readers this amounts to a practical prohibition. Xerography has not yet made its appearance in Russian libraries. Finally, the Russian reader does not have the alternative of buying a copy of the book for himself. Except for publications of foreign Communist presses, no foreign books are for sale in the Soviet Union other than, in second-hand bookstores, the few that somehow trickle in. These bring astronomical prices: the equivalent of $60.00 for a worn copy of *Webster's Collegiate Dictionary,* $10.00 for a used American paperback. Since the Russian ruble is inconvertible in the Western currency market, the ordinary citizen cannot simply write to England or America and order a book. Even if Soviet postal authorities would allow the order to go through, the Russian would have no way of making payment. High-ranking scholars are provided with a foreign currency allowance which they may use to order books and journal subscriptions from abroad; the ordinary student or professor is not. As a result, even the Soviet specialist in some area of research will not have an adequate library of foreign works in his field. A logician will have heard of but never seen Whitehead and Russell's *Principia Mathematica*. A specialist in American pragmatism will not own John Dewey's *Experience and Nature*.

Subject to these limitations, specialized work in philosophy on the graduate level is also carried on in greater range and depth than was possible during the Stalin era. Depending upon his initiative and his field of special interest, the Russian graduate student may, at least in some cases, be engaged in advanced work in philosophy indistinguishable from the work of his counterpart in an American university.

During the academic year 1964-1965, the Philosophy Faculty of Moscow University had 254 postgraduate degree candidates. Of these, eight or nine—plus many laboratory workers who are not considered degree candidates—worked in the Psychology Division of the Philosophy Faculty, and thirty to thirty-five in the Division of Scientific Communism, a new unit established to produce philosophers with better knowledge of the concrete problems of creating the new Communist society. The remaining graduate students were enrolled in the Philosophy Division proper. This division, which thus includes the great majority of graduate students in the Philosophy Faculty, is itself divided into a number of departments, each with its own faculty, chairman and departmental office. Each graduate student works in one of these departments. There are separate departments for the two major branches of Marxist-Leninist philosophy—dialectical materialism and historical materialism. Three departments are devoted to the history of philosophy: the history of "foreign" (almost exclusively Western) philosophy, the history of Russian (prerevolutionary) philosophy and the history of Marxist-Leninist philosophy. In addition there is a department of logic, a department of aesthetics and ethics—largely confined, in practice, to aesthetics—and a department of "the history and theory of atheism and religion."

Ordinarily the student has worked or been in military service for two or more years before beginning graduate study (he may begin at any age up to thirty-five), and in such a case receives from the State a stipend of $111 a month, an income higher than most factory workers. In the rare cases in which a student comes directly from undergraduate work, the stipend is only $77. All graduate students are accommodated in a university dormitory if their families do not live in Moscow—another boon in a society of short housing. During their first year they take required seminars in dialectical and historical materialism. The next two years are free of course requirements, and are spent on writing a dissertation. The dissertation must be completed within the three-year program. In any event the graduate student leaves residence and his stipend is discontinued after three years, but the great majority of dissertations are completed within that period. The degree received is that of "Candidate of Philosophical Sciences." The highest degree, a doctorate, is awarded only to established scholars upon presentation and defense of a major dissertation, usually not less than five years after formal graduate work has been completed with the earning of the "Candidate" degree.

The almost total freedom from course requirements in the graduate program contrasts sharply with the heavy load of the undergraduate, and on the whole the program cannot be considered particularly demanding. Dissertation standards are not always high. In practice the dissertation is begun and completed during the third year in many cases, so that the student has considerable leisure during the first and second years. The graduate student does have other duties, however. He is considered a non-teaching member of his department, and participates in its meetings. Thus he takes part in making department policy and discussing his fellows' dissertations. He also assists in examining undergraduates. He may do some teaching as well, for which he receives extra compensation.

The character and quality of the work done by the graduate student varies greatly from department to department and student to student. One of the larger departments, the Department of the History and Theory of Atheism and Religion, no doubt owes its popularity (it has about thirty graduate students) at least in part to the abundance of well paying teaching jobs in this field for degree holders; every Soviet institution of higher learning has a required course in atheism. An additional attraction for some students is that they find the work in this department relatively easy. "There are no difficult problems here," one explained, "after all, there is no God." Even in this department, however, officially dedicated to disseminating the truth of atheism and exposing the errors of religion, it is possible for a student to do respectable work on topics like those which might engage a Western student of theology or the philosophy or history of religion. A recent candidate, working on what he described as "evangelical theology," was reading John A. T. Robinson's *Honest to God* and studying the views of Niebuhr, Bultmann and Tillich. Another was investigating the policies of the papacy between the two world wars. A third was writing a dissertation entitled "The Concept of Freedom in Contemporary Neo-Thomism." All this work was being done within the framework of Soviet Marxism, and would in its final form begin with appropriate quotations from Lenin and end with Marxist criticism. But its substance might be solid and in some respect original. (One Soviet professor commented: "You Western scholars read only the first few pages and the last few pages of our books and find them hackneyed and biased. You ought to read what comes in between.")

The largest department, the Department of Dialectical Materialism, likewise benefits from the availability of teaching positions for its graduates. But it also has a greater reputation for challenging and substantial work, particularly in the philosophy of science. A number of its younger faculty members are known for pioneering work on problems within Marxist philosophy hitherto largely bypassed by Soviet scholars: problems concerning the nature of change, the origin of life, the question of whether philosophy is an ideology or a science. These faculty members are publishing studies and directing the dissertations of graduate students in these areas.

Another department, the Department of the History of Foreign Philosophy, had in 1964-1965 only six graduate students. Work in this department is thought generally to be more demanding than work in others, requiring, for one thing, a good knowledge of foreign languages. And in Soviet institutions of higher learning there is less demand for teachers of the history of Western philosophy. Of the nine regular faculty members of this department, six are concerned chiefly with contemporary Western philosophy. A number of the recent books most highly regarded by Soviet philosophers for rigorous and incisive analysis have come from this staff: V. F. Asmus' *The Problem of Intuition in Philosophy and Mathematics* (1963), A. S. Bogomolov's *The Idea of Development in Bourgeois Philosophy of the Nineteenth and Twentieth Centuries* (1962), P. P. Gaydenko's *Existentialism and the Problem of Culture: A Critique of the Philosophy of M. Heidegger* (1962) and I. S. Narsky's works on contemporary British and American analytic philosophy. Their graduate students pursue comparable topics, generally with a contemporary emphasis. Thus a graduate student in this department might be working on the philosophical anthropology of Max Scheler and more recent German thinkers, or on the philosophy of A. J. Ayer or the later Wittgenstein, and might have, allowing for his limited access to materials, as good an understanding of them as a comparable specialist in the West. What is more, he would be capable of talking about them technically and comprehensively, without reference to Marxism. Indeed in some cases, perhaps through considerations of prudence or diplomacy, he would actually resist relating them to Marxism in a discussion with a foreign visitor.

If this degree of informed interest in Western philosophy is still exceptional among Soviet students, it is surely less exceptional than it was ten years ago. The interest extends even to curiosity about the personal lives of the Western thinkers the young Russian philosophers have come increasingly to know. ("Where does Rudolf Carnap live? Is he married?") A bizarre rumor circulated in the Philosophy Faculty in 1965 to the effect that Bertrand Russell had become a convert to the Baptist faith. Understandably the interest has outstripped the information. One straight-A undergraduate in philosophy said: "I would very much like to know more about your leading American philosophers, such as Santayana, Dewey and F. Scott Fitzgerald."

Another sign of increasing philosophical vitality in the Soviet Union are the specialized conferences which have been organized in the past few years. Of particular interest are those focused on Western philosophical movements which would largely have been ignored or abused, rather than examined seriously, during the Stalin era. In 1963 a major conference involving Soviet academicians and leading philosophers from all over the country was held on the subject, "Sign and Meaning." It was devoted to an examination of contemporary analytic philosophy in the West. In November, 1964, an analogous conference on "Marxism and Existentialism" was held in Moscow, sponsored by the Philosophy Faculty of Moscow University.

In the latter conference seven major papers and ten briefer reports were read in a two-day period, all (except the opening paper by Academician M. B. Mitin) by professors and graduate students of Moscow University. The conference was much talked about in advance and was attended each day by between one hundred and one hundred and fifty persons, most of them from the Philosophy Faculty. The papers varied greatly in substance and tone, ranging from stock denunciations of existentialism as expressing the moral decay of capitalist society to informative technical analyses of existentialist concepts. As the papers varied, so did the reaction of the audience. The more primitive the approach, the less attention the audience gave the speaker. As if enduring a boring and unwelcome ritual, they talked with one another in conversational tones, moved in and out of the room, sometimes even gave the speaker good-natured catcalls and a thumbs-down gesture. As the substance of the papers increased, so did the attention of the audience, to the point where a difficult, rapid-fire analysis of Heidegger's concept of time (which concluded with the observation that Heidegger is one of the most significant thinkers of the present day) was greeted with total attention and vigorous note-taking. Many of the speakers complained of the "mystifications" of the existentialists, and in balance the tone of the conference was decidedly negative. Yet there was much responsible and informed discussion of the philosophical significance of the category of the "irrational," of the Russian émigré existentialists Shestov and Berdyaev, of the concept of alienation from Hegel to Kafka and Marcel—all subjects that would hardly have been discussed ten years ago.

At the end of the first day's session a member of the audience, a well-known local gadfly who had been imprisoned under Stalin, asked for and was granted permission to speak from the rostrum. Angrily and excitedly he charged that most of the scheduled speakers were still proceeding "as if Marxists have a monopoly on the truth." Existentialism, he contended, is not exclusively a product of bourgeois society, as some of the speakers had claimed, but instead results from a spiritual climate present also in the Soviet Union. "There are dark forces in our own society," he asserted, with references to the Stalin era. The audience greeted his comments with mingled amusement and uneasiness, and there was no discussion of them. But he was not interrupted, or denounced when he had finished.

In addition to taking part in these Soviet conferences, Russian philosophers are also increasingly venturing out to philosophical conferences in other parts of the world. Typically the Soviet delegation, upon its return home, reports on the proceedings at open meetings.

Audiences for Western philosophers within the Soviet Union are still almost nonexistent, however. The English philosopher A. J. Ayer was invited to lecture in Moscow and Leningrad in 1962. In the same year, an article by Ayer, with appropriate Soviet commentary, was published in *Voprosy filosofii.* The present writer, while a participant in the cultural exchange program between the United States and the Soviet Union during the academic year 1964-1965, was asked to present three papers on nineteenth century Russian philosophy to the faculty and graduate students of the Department of the History of Russian Philosophy at Moscow University—a courtesy not demanded by the conditions of the exchange. The papers, written from a non-Marxist point of view, were criticized vigorously but seriously and politely. But these are isolated instances. In general the non-Marxist Westerner is all but excluded from direct confrontation with a Soviet audience. No international conferences of philosophy have yet been held in the Soviet Union.

Philosophy, the most sensitive of the intellectual disciplines in the Soviet Union, has on the whole fared well in the process of de-Stalinization which began with the Twentieth Party Congress in 1956. It has suffered no such dramatic setbacks as occurred in art with the outbursts of Chairman Khrushchev in 1962, or more recently in literature with the Siniavsky-Daniel trial and the high-level criticism of some literary journals for departing from the canons of socialist realism.* Perhaps this is because philosophy has yet progressed so little and so slowly. The key tenets of Marxist-Leninist philosophy are still regarded as an unquestionable framework within which the Soviet philosopher must operate, and these tenets are still in fact considerably more demanding than the simple assertions that "matter is primary" and "the world is knowable."

Yet the charges which have occurred are such as give promise of further development in the future. They may be summed up conveniently under four headings: first, the increased availability of works by non-Marxist philosophers and of information concerning philosophical alternatives to Marxism, both past and present; second, an increasingly professional spirit which values rigorous and responsible analysis over the militant abuse which previously dominated the Soviet treatment of opposing views; third, the legitimization of philosophical investigation in some areas, such as formal logic and cybernetics, which previously were rejected as valueless and inconsistent with dialectical materialism; fourth, increased attention to particular problems which arise within the framework of dialectical materialism, particularly problems in the philosophy of science. All these trends give evidence of an increased willingness to tolerate disagreement and genuine discussion. Considerable obstacles still confront progress in this direction, above all the continuing, if diminished, insularity of Soviet philosophy. Formidable bars still hinder the introduction of both foreign books and foreign scholars to the Soviet audience. But the present trends, if continued, will work to diminish this insularity still further.

* It is feared, however, that the recently reported arrest in March, 1967, of some twenty-five professors and students of philosophy at Leningrad University signifies such a setback.

# 7

---

## The Politics of Soviet Culture: 1964-1967

### TIMOTHY McCLURE

It is one of the ironies of the Soviet system that the Communist party has built anti-intellectualism into its structure and outlook, yet finds itself ever more dependent on scientists, economists, writers and even artists. The Party has tried to isolate the intellectuals by giving them a privileged position in society and at the same time controlling their output through an elaborate network of organizations and censors. But with the inevitable development of a more open and complex Soviet society, the Party, its creature organizations, and the intellectuals have found themselves in a multisided tug-of-war—a struggle in which strange alliances develop, and it often becomes impossible to tell the "good guys" from the "bad guys."

The tension resulting from this struggle has not as yet stimulated great cultural achievement; on the contrary, it has resulted in an enormous dissipation of intellectual energy and waste of talent. Yet out of the articulation of the conflict has become a meaningful dialogue, forcing the Establishment along a course that has vacillated between grappling with the crucial question of greater free-

---

This article originally appeared in **Problems of Communism**, vol. XVI, no. 2 (March-April, 1967), and is reproduced with their permission. "Timothy McClure" is the pseudonym of an observer of Soviet affairs who has been a frequent visitor to the Soviet Union over the past ten years.

dom and reverting to the search for more effective ways to control and discipline the intellectuals. The trial of the two Soviet writers Siniavski and Daniel in February, 1966, marked the latest stormy effort at discipline in the cycle of tempest and relative calm that has characterized the relationship between intellectuals and the regime since Stalin's death.

The "crisis of the intellectuals" in 1965-66 had much in common with the 1963 crackdown on the arts, which began with the bizarre visit of Khrushchev to the Manezh art exhibit on December 1, 1962, but dissipated only six months later with the June, 1963, ideological plenum of the CPSU Central Committee.[1] During both periods the heightened debate between "liberal" and "conservative" writers served as a surrogate battlefield for contending forces within the Establishment and most likely within the Central Committee and the Politburo itself. In both periods, also, the authorities finally backed away from the threatened general repression of the liberals in the official family, while the liberals in turn felt vindicated and emboldened to risk even more daring excursions into artistic experimentation and social criticism. Furthermore, in 1963, as in 1966, the repressive actions that were sanctioned by the Party resulted in an outpouring of shocked disapproval and indignation from foreign intellectuals, most particularly from Communists in Eastern and Western Europe.

At the same time, there are significant differences between the two periods of "crackdown," revealing a good deal about current Soviet politics and about the quality and extent of intellectual dissidence in Soviet society. One striking difference concerns the target of attack: in the 1962-63 crisis it was the young poets and the liberal wing of the official intelligentsia that bore the brunt of the leadership's wrath, whereas in 1966 the Soviet authorities directed their major effort against intellectuals who had sought to circumvent the Party's controls by operating in the intellectual underground. Partly in consequence, official retaliation was more severe in 1966, resulting in stiff prison sentences for at least two Soviet writers (and subsequently many more) and in the expulsion

[1] For a comprehensive review of this period, see Priscilla Johnson, "The Regime and the Intellectuals: A Window on Party Politics," *Problems of Communism,* Special Supplement, July-August, 1963.

from the country of a third writer critical of the regime. Yet meanwhile the targets of the 1962-63 crackdown were left relatively unmolested and even flourishing; what fire these by-now-not-so-young writers and poets drew from the literary and bureaucratic conservatives served in large part merely to increase the demand for their publications and to make them even more inviolable institutions in Soviet society.

Another distinction between the two crises concerns the behavior of the top political leadership. The first crisis grew out of an impetuous political *volte-face* by Khrushchev at his most erratic and irascible, and his person continued to dominate the events that ensued. By contrast, during the 1966 crisis the leaders managed to stay out of direct involvement with the intellectuals and to leave the dirty work to lesser agents. Moreover, the decision to put Siniavski and Daniel on trial, risking the further alienation of the Soviet liberal intellectuals and universal disapproval from abroad, was surely not an easy or impetuous move on the part of the cautious coalition of Khrushchev's successors, who were otherwise demonstrating a desire to legitimize their right to rule and displaying a high degree of sensitivity to foreign criticism. The decision that seemed to be so atypical for Khrushchev's heirs must have reflected, as Max Hayward observed, a leadership "torn between powerful conflicting trends, and attempting to placate, or at least not to antagonize, violently opposed groups in Soviet society, if not in the party itself." [2]

In the following pages a closer look will be taken at the events surrounding the recent crisis, though neither the trial itself nor the writings of Siniavski and Daniel will be dealt with in detail since these matters have already been covered extensively. [3] For the purpose of analyzing the changing policies of Khrushchev's heirs it has been convenient to divide the time since Khrushchev's fall into roughly three phases: (1) the period of uncertainty from mid-

[2] *On Trial: The Soviet State versus "Abram Tertz" and "Nikolai Arzhak"* (translated, edited, and with an introduction by Max Hayward) (New York: Harper & Row, 1966), p. 38.

[3] E.g., see Leopold Labedz and Max Hayward, "The Arrests," and Abraham Brumberg, "Traitors in the Dock," *Problems of Communism*, March-April, 1966. (The Labedz-Hayward article was reprinted from *Encounter* [London], January, 1966.)

October, 1964, to mid-January, 1965, during which the party
leadership was too bothered with disestablishing Khrushchevism
and establishing its own *bona fides* in the Communist world to
concern itself with cultural matters; (2) the period of "liberal
conservatism" from late January to mid-summer, 1965, during
which certain elements in the leadership were able to make important, if only moderate, overtures to encourage the intellectuals'
participation in developing new programs and in expanding the
arts; and (3) the period of reaction and disciplinary measures
from September, 1965, through 1967. In the conclusion the political implications of the crackdown will be examined.

One note: Throughout this essay reference is made to the various
segments of the intelligentsia as "liberals," "moderates," "conservatives," "liberal-conservatives," to designate their political stance in
the struggle between forces that seek and forces that oppose a more
open society in the Soviet Union. Such designations are necessary
and valid within the context of the essay, but they perforce ignore
the rich variety and multitude of crosscurrents that characterize the
climate of cultural opinion within the intellectual community.

By October, 1964, the liberal writers and artists—most of
whom had wisely chosen the "conspiracy of silence" during the
conservative onslaught of 1963—had reemerged from the provinces and dachas and had actively resumed the game of who can
publish what and where. A certain confidence was in the air in
Moscow. The broadcasts of VOA and BBC had not been jammed
for over a year. The year-old Nuclear Test Ban Treaty plus angry
exchanges with the Chinese pointed to even closer relations with
the West in the coming year—a development welcomed by the vast
majority of the Soviet intelligentsia. The atmosphere in Moscow
seemed so hopeful that the visiting Yugoslav, Mihajlo Mihajlov,
despite his pessimistic view of Soviet society in general, saw light
ahead for Soviet artists: in his *Moscow Summer, 1964,* he pre-
dicted "a final liberation of literature and arts from all restrictions
of dogmatism"—a surprising judgment from such a knowledgeable
observer, but certainly a reflection of the naive optimism that prevailed at the time among the younger intellectuals.

This air of general well-being was rudely jolted by the announcement of Khrushchev's fall on October 16. The immediate

reaction of the intellectual community and probably of most citizens was understandably one of misgiving and uncertainty, but concern over what lay ahead no doubt outweighed concern over the change of regime *per se*. Among the intellectuals, the liberals' reactions were the most confused, for they had long felt ambivalent toward Khrushchev. They all knew that Khrushchev had been the first to open the floodgates of denunciation against Stalin; that he had personally authorized the publication of *One Day in the Life of Ivan Denisovich* and *The Heirs of Stalin;* that he had seemed impressed by certain independent artists like the sculptor Ernst Neizvestny and the poet Yevtushenko (both of whom had shown the bravado to talk back to the top man himself). On the other hand, Khrushchev's crude, peasant approach to culture had epitomized the Party's philistinism and purely utilitarian view of art, and it was he who had placed the control of culture in the hands of the dogmatic and detested Ilichev. Furthermore, though Khrushchev had initiated de-Stalinization, he had resisted yielding to its logical demands; indeed, as First Secretary, he had wielded his authority in the Stalinist style, making himself the final arbiter in all aspects of Soviet life.

Even more than the writers and artists, the scientific intelligentsia had reasons not to feel overly regretful about Khrushchev's downfall. Perhaps no segment of the Soviet Establishment had been more contemptuous of his pretensions to expert knowledge and his various crash programs. The scientists were particularly antagonized by his often enthusiastic support for the charlatan geneticist Lysenko—an issue on which the liberals in the "creative intelligentsia" were solidly in agreement.

Thus a few reassuring developments under the new regime were enough to quiet the initial misgivings of the intelligentsia. Nothing could have offered quicker comfort than the post-Khrushchev attack launched in the press against Lysenko, his theories and his supporters; an article by Vladimir Dudintsev published in *Komsomolskaia pravda* on October 23, only a week after Khrushchev's ouster, sparked an outpouring of abuse against Lysenko over the next few weeks that seemed clearly designed to win the support of the intelligentsia.

Also within a week of the ouster, word was passed that the

authorities had dropped Khrushchev's pending project to combine the major literary and cultural newspapers into one organ.[4] This was another easy way to win support from all sectors of the intellectual community, each of which had a stake in its own particular publication. The release of Pasternak's close friend, Olga Ivinskaia, from prison in early November (very possibly because she had already served out her sentence) was another means of picking up goodwill from the liberals. Word was also floated that the young Leningrad poet, Yosif Brodski, had been released from his place of exile near Archangel, where he had been sent six months earlier by a Leningrad court for "parasitism"—but this rumor later turned out to be false.[5]

Among other signs encouraging to the liberals, *Pravda,* newly under the editorship of A. M. Rumiantsev, took to criticizing the conservative playwright, A. Sofranov, and the conservative stronghold, *Oktiabr.*[6] On November 30, Yevgeni Yevtushenko, Bella Akhmadulina and Rimma Kazakova—three of the leading young liberals—gave a poetry reading to some 1,800 people in the Moscow Conservatory, the first such large reading by the liberal poets since the events of 1962-63. In late December, "Poetry Day" saw most of the liberal poets reading to small audiences.

All of these developments, however, were more or less wisps in the wind—or one might better say in the partial vacuum created by the turnover in the top leadership. Khrushchev's heirs had not as yet enunciated any official line in the sphere of culture—indeed in the first few months they showed little interest in the problems of the "culture lobby." They were concerned with the more pressing problems of tidying up the structural aberrations in the Party, reassuring the nation's bureaucrats that they could rule better and more securely without that "subjectivist" Khrushchev, and mending fences with friends in the Communist movement. Cultural life seemed to proceed as usual in Moscow and Leningrad, reflecting— in many respects—trends that had been underway before Khrushchev's fall.

[4] This was later confirmed by a speaker at the RSFSR Writers' Congress in March, 1965.

[5] Brodski was finally allowed to return to Leningrad in November, 1965.

[6] See "Where Is the Compass?," *Pravda,* November 15, 1964.

The first clear sign that some official sanction was being given to a moderate direction in cultural policies came with significant shake-ups in the literary and scientific bureaucracies. In late January, 1965, the Moscow and Leningrad sections of the Writers' Union met in stormy sessions, with dramatic results. The Moscow meeting was highlighted by indirect but unmistakable criticism of Ilichev, the chief of the Party's Ideological Commission, and of the hack writer Nikolai Gribachev, who had thundered as one of the major conservative voices in 1963. The Moscow writers succeeded in removing from their directing board four of the most despised representatives of the old guard: besides Gribachev, they were *Oktiabr's* editor, Vsevolod Kochetov, the playwright Anatoli Sofronov, and the writer Georgi Markov. The four also failed to win election as delegates from Moscow to the upcoming RSFSR Writers' Congress, forcing them—as in 1962—to retire to the provinces where they could be assured of inclusion in other delegations. In Leningrad a similar triumph was scored: the Stalinist poet Aleksandr Prokofiev was not only removed as First Secretary of the Leningrad Writers' Union but was denied a seat on the new board and strongly criticized for his report to the meeting. Prokofiev was the symbol of old guard control over Leningrad's writers and had reportedly been the key advocate of harsh treatment for Brodski less than a year earlier.

The next straw in the wind was the report of M. A. Keldish, President of the Soviet Union's Academy of Sciences, to a February 1 meeting of the Academy, in which he officially condemned Lysenkoism and its negative effect on the development of biological and related sciences. The Keldish report (printed in *Pravda,* Feb. 4) was supported, as it turned out, by an earlier unpublished Party-government decree on improving biology; the removal of Lysenko and his cronies from positions of power in genetics and in the biological and agricultural sciences became a foregone conclusion.

By mid-February there were other indicators suggesting that the moderately liberal line issued from the top party leadership—or at least an influential element of it: changes in the RSFSR Institute of Pedagogical Sciences and the formation of a new educational commission gave real hope that professionals would have a major voice in the restructuring of education, following the reversal of Khrushchev's ill-fated reforms. Similarly the economists, long isolated from policy-making, found themselves—to their great surprise—being approached for concrete proposals in anticipation of the overdue economic reforms that had been much discussed in Khrushchev's last years.

On February 21, *Pravda* published an editorial, over the signature of its new editor, Rumiantsev, that seemed to herald a more enlightened period of cooperation between the Party and the intellectuals. At long last the regime seemed to be recognizing that the economists, scientists and writers could be of real value to the Party if they were allowed experimentation, open disagreement, competition and considerable freedom. While the editorial clearly reasserted the primacy of the Party, it appeared to represent an official view that might best be described as "liberal conservative" —a view implicitly acknowledging that the Party's periodic confrontations with the increasingly influential cultural and scientific lobbies could only discredit the Party itself and cause waste in the society. Among other key passages, Rumiantsev stated that it was necessary "to learn how . . . to open the road to everything talented and socially useful created by Soviet scientists and figures in culture and literature." And he declared: ". . . genuine creation is possible only in an environment of search, experiment, and the free expression and collision of opinions, the presence of various schools and trends, various styles and genres competing among themselves and at the same time joined by the unity of . . . Socialist Realism." This was certainly a novel definition of Socialist Realism!

On the same weekend that the Rumiantsev editorial appeared, *Novyi mir's* first issue of 1965 hit the newsstands, and it seemed to provide proof that the liberal lobby was to be given wide leeway. In the lead article poet-editor Tvardovski stated more emphatically and openly than perhaps ever before his magazine's liberal position on the arts and belief in the artist's right to express his "small truth."

Only a month later the March plenum of the CPSU Central Committee announced the demotion of L. F. Ilichev from his position as ideological boss of the Secretariat to a lesser role as a Deputy Minister of Foreign Affairs. Ilichev's place was taken by Piotr Demichev, who had been Party Secretary for the Chemical Industry under Khrushchev but who was promoted in November, 1964, to the Politburo. From his earlier days in the Moscow city party organization, Demichev was known to be more moderate on cultural matters than Ilichev, and his first informal meetings with small groups of writers confirmed that he would be far less likely to meddle directly in their affairs than his predecessor.

As the long winter gradually gave way to spring, all these developments combined to nurture a growing sense of optimism among the liberals and moderates in the intelligentsia. At the same time, there were other developments that perhaps should have been recognized as harbingers of another sort of winter. The RSFSR Writers' Congress in March brought cold solace to the liberals, as the conservative bureaucrats from the provinces vented their spleen on young writers in seeming sharp violation of the Rumiantsev line. The most ominous sounds came from Moscow party boss Yegorychev, who declared that the obsession of certain writers with the mistakes of the Stalin era "casts a shadow over the holy of holies—our socialist organization, Marxist-Leninist teaching, and the general line of the Party." His call for less criticism of the Soviet past was a line that would be heard with increasing regularity and vigor over the coming months. Indeed, an effort to curb anti-Stalinist influences had already been evidenced by a significant decrease in the number of rehabilitations of the victims of Stalin's purges. The propaganda buildup for the May 9 celebrations of the twentieth anniversary of VE Day was accompanied by the first public mention in years of Stalin in a positive vein. On May 8, Brezhnev himself uttered the terrible name, and the steely visage appeared on Moscow TV and in a documentary film on the war which was shown in Moscow.

This hint of a Stalinist revival, coexisting with the fresh sense of freedom among intellectuals—both following on the partial vacuum in cultural controls that was created by Khrushchev's ouster —resulted in a peculiarly restive and exciting atmosphere in the spring of 1965. In the arts, it had been the best season in years—

there were two new experimental theaters in Moscow, and the plays of Berthold Brecht had burst on the stages of Moscow and Leningrad with full force. Voznesenski's "Oza" had dazzled both his admirers and his critics with its "formalist" tendencies. In April Yevtushenko's lengthy poem, "Bratsk Dam," a restatement of many of his controversial themes, appeared in *Yunost*. *Novyi mir* outreached itself in its first six issues of the new year, particularly with the two tender and penetrating novels on rural life, *The Mayfly's Life is Short* by Vladimir Tendriakov (May issue), and *Seven in One House* by Vitali Siomin (June issue). *Yunost's* anniversary issue in June featured the young poets as well as a new story by prose writer Vasili Aksionov, whose play, *Always on Sale,* which had premiered in the spring at the Sovremennik Theater, marked the first important step by a modern Soviet playwright into the field of fantastic satire. And a new collection of Boris Pasternak's poetry was assigned to the press with an introduction by the devoted Pasternak scholar—Andrei Siniavski.

Even more striking than the quality of Soviet writing was the significant breakthrough in the foreign literature published in this period. For the first time, Kafka's short stories appeared in Russian; Faulkner's trilogy was finally put out in large editions; John Updike's *The Centaur* became the talk of literary Moscow after publication in *Inostrannaia literatura,* and a host of other major foreign writers began to appear in print. All of which suggested that the cultural "opening up" of Soviet society was a fact of life which neither the party bureaucrats nor the conservatives predominating in the publishing world could significantly retard.

The most unusual development was the degree to which young intellectuals and students were expressing themselves openly—aggressively showing, as one Soviet writer said, that they were the first Soviet generation "without the habit of fear." On April 14, 1965, a young organization of dissident poets, the *Smogisti,*[7] marched from Maiakovski Square to the Writers' Union Club on

[7] The term *Smog* is derived from the first letters of the Russian words *slovo* (word), *mysl* (thought), *obraz* (form), *glubina* (profundity). Some reports have the "S" standing for *smelost* (courage). The Soviet press has tried to disparage the *Smogisti* by saying the term stands for the "Very Youngest Society of Geniuses."

Herzen Street, where they stood blocking traffic and reciting their unorthodox verse, to the utter amazement of Union officials who had neither seen nor heard of an unauthorized demonstration of Soviet citizens in Moscow for years. Another remarkable occurrence took place in the spring at a large organized student meeting at Moscow University; a young speaker who was ostensibly on the platform to condemn "Western bourgeois cynicism" for invoking the statute of limitations on Nazi war criminals in West Germany, shocked his audience by proclaiming that the real cynics were the leaders of the Soviet Union, who had revealed the horrible crimes of the Stalin era but had as yet failed to bring any of the perpetrators to trial.

It was also in the spring of 1965 that the eminent Ilya Ehrenburg, speaking to a group of writers at Moscow's Foreign Literature Library, declared that the time had passed when writers should describe how they suffered under Stalin—that they should now begin examining the question of "how Stalinism could have happened."

Looking back, the spring of 1965 seems to have been a period in which the leadership was perforce acting in a collective manner while groping for coherent programs—and for a more stable leadership alliance. In the process of developing such programs the new regime seemed more willing than its predecessor to turn for help to various segments of the intelligentsia. Thus, as it turned out, this period of "liberal conversatism" was not a policy line set down by the party leadership, but the result of several converging phenomena—a reaction to the excesses of Khrushchev's leadership style, the articulation by at least a segment of the party leadership (through Rumiantsev) of a moderate long-range approach to the intelligentsia, and the bolder action of liberal and young intellectuals encouraged by the apparent relaxation and increasingly confident of their cause. As viewed by the Party, however, the "new conservatism" called for a strict limitation on writings or discussion that disparaged the Stalin era or the role of the Party and the secret police in that era. In return, the liberals were to be allowed more opportunity to experiment with style and to be spared excessive attacks from their conservative critics.

The partial moratorium on heavy-handed conservative criticism was short-lived. By late July and August the conservative critics had opened up on their favorite targets—Aksionov, Voznesenski, Tendriakov and Yevtushenko—and had found a new one in Vitali Siomin, whose aforementioned novel, *Seven in One House,* was the literary sensation of the season. *Pravda* printed a strong attack on Siomin, charging that he had dealt only with the "private truths" of a small group of isolated individuals and thereby distorted the big truth—the balanced picture—of Soviet reality. The issue of the "small" or "foxhole truth" versus the universal or big truth had been central in the liberal-conservative debate, particularly since the fall of Khrushchev. The liberals maintained that the private truth (*istina*) of the artist did not necessarily conflict with the big truth (*pravda*)—and that anyway it was the prerogative of a Communist artist to express his personal view of reality. This aspect of the debate also involved the issue of de-Stalinization—i.e., whether the revelation of individual crimes of the Stalin period distorted the entire reality of Soviet life. The cultural conservatives and many in the Party obviously thought that it did.

The young prose writer, Vasili Aksionov, also drew major fire from the orthodox literary critics. The most serious attack came in *Izvestia* (August 13) which followed up a letter from irate taxi drivers in Yalta (the subject of a recent Aksionov story) with an editorial comment castigating all Soviet writers who painted a gloomy— and ergo distorted—picture of Soviet life. The *Izvestia* editors criticized the liberal journals, *Novyi mir* and *Yunost* specifically, an unusual move even during the worst of times for Soviet writers.

Having been given the green light by *Izvestia* and seemingly by *Pravda,* the conservatives wasted no time in using their preponderant control over the literary journals and newspapers to focus on what they saw as the recent insidious trends in prose, poetry, drama and films. Finally—as if to give the official seal of approval of the young party leaders to the conservative resurgence— *Komsomol* chief S. P. Pavlov, writing in *Pravda* (August 27), blamed certain journals and theaters for the malaise apparent among some Soviet youth and exhorted the Party's literary critics to be more harsh in judging such "trash." Most significant, Pavlov called for a revival of the atmosphere of the nineteen-thirties among the *Komsomols* and explained how the police, the army, the border guards and DOSAAF had all recently instituted new programs to restore respect among *Komsomols* for past Soviet military glories. At this juncture Rumiantsev published his second *Pravda* editorial (September 9), which in a highly polemical tone responded to the recent intemperance of conservative critics. In an almost unprecedented act, Rumiantsev reprimanded the government newspaper *Izvestia* (as well as the party agricultural newspaper *Selskaia zhizn*) for assaulting the liberal writers and journals. He strongly restated his case that the Party needed to trust intellectuals and allow them more freedom for growth. In support of the liberal cause on the question of "private truths," Rumiantsev pointed out that it is "unrealistic to expect from an author absolute universality—with such a demand we wouldn't receive any artistic works," suggesting by implication that he also supported the continued examination of the errors of Stalin. Even more striking than his attack on the government newspapers was his charge that any effort "to place in opposition such concepts as intellectuality, party-mindedness, and popular-mindedness represents a dogmatic and stupid argument against a scientific world outlook," leading to the same type of arbitrary and crude direction of society for which the Party had removed Khrushchev.

Just four days prior to Rumiantsev's article *Pravda* (September 5) had carried an editorial on the nationality question which recalled, for the first time since the early postwar years, Lenin's demand for a constant "struggle against anti-Semitism." [8] In Soviet society the Jewish question inevitably comes to the forefront during periods of heightened anti-intellectualism, as it most certainly did during 1962-63. What was clearly at issue in the early days of September, 1965, then, was the growing atmosphere of anti-intellectualism, the mounting pressures to reevaluate the Stalin era,

[8] On July 19, *Pravda* had also printed the text of a speech delivered by Premier Kosygin in Riga, in which he condemned anti-Semitism. It was interestingly enough Kosygin again who, at a press conference in Paris on December 3, 1966, implied that Soviet Jews could emigrate to unite families, thus making him appear as one of the "liberals" on the Jewish question. No other top leaders have addressed this matter publicly.

and the conservative demands for more attention to the purification of ideology and the increase of discipline in society.

It was in this setting that Siniavski and Daniel were arrested in the second week of September. Some nine or ten days later Rumiantsev was removed as Editor-in-Chief of *Pravda*.[9] That the two events were connected seemed patently clear.

Although Rumiantsev reportedly had been ailing, no such reason was given for his replacement less than a year after he had assumed the office. Furthermore, he appeared well enough to resume an active role in other fields within a month. Whether or not he personally wrote the editorials in defense of greater intellectual freedom, their appearance over his name had publicly identified him with the most moderate semi-official approach to the intelligentsia since the pre-Stalin era. Thus his removal suggested strongly that either the cultural line was changing or that Rumiantsev was involved in a squabble of the highest order—or both.

There are very good reasons to assume that the pressures against the Rumiantsev moderate line were mounting anyway, but the Siniavski-Daniel case most certainly gave added weight to the conservative thrust and may conceivably have been used to precipitate the crisis. The arrest of the two writers—for publishing abroad "slanderous" literature about the Soviet state—was at the least, timely from the conservatives' point of view. While it may seem astonishing that the KGB, with its network of informers and controls on foreign visitors, did not have some earlier clue to the writers' contacts, the evidence suggests that their activities went undetected until the spring or summer of 1965.[10] In any event, this was the final "proof" the conservatives needed to support their

[9] According to letters signed by their wives and later published abroad, Siniavski was arrested on September 8 and Daniel on September 12. See *Grani* (Frankfurt), No. 62, November, 1966. On September 21, TASS announced that M. V. Zimianin had replaced Rumiantsev as the Editor-in-Chief of *Pravda*.

[10] The text of the trial implies that the bugging of Siniavski's apartment began in the summer of 1965 (cf. *On Trial . . . , supra*). It seems highly unlikely that Khrushchev would have passed up the chance to throw Siniavski to the wolves in 1962-63—or that the authorities would have permitted him to play such a key role in defending the liberal cause in 1964-65—had they known of his activities.

case that the intellectuals could not be trusted. The Party felt indignant and betrayed.

The developments directly related to the trial need little review, since so much has been written about the case. Suffice it to say that throughout the fall and into January of 1966, the crucial issue for Soviet intellectuals became the fate of the two arrested writers. Some members of the official intelligentsia felt that the offenders should not be put on trial but should instead be turned over to the writers' organization for appropriate punishment—as was done in the Pasternak case. On the other hand, 200 Moscow students who demonstrated in Pushkin Square on December 5 (Soviet "Constitution Day") demanded a trial—but one that was fair and open as required by Soviet law. Protests and appeals poured into the Soviet authorities from foreign intellectuals on behalf of the two writers.

On January 13, *Izvestia* published a viciously slanderous article against the writers, setting the stage for all ensuing propaganda and for the trial itself. The accusations in official Soviet newspapers seemed almost incredibly prejudicial to Western observers, and must have been totally disheartening to Soviet citizens who had been hoping for legal "guarantees" of their rights.

The macabre trial opened on a grey February morning in a small Moscow court building. It was not an open trial in that only a chosen few were issued tickets to attend. The text of the proceedings that was subsequently smuggled out and published abroad revealed a classic confrontation between two sensitive intellectuals and a frightened, philistine Establishment.[11] Daniel pointed out the irony of a powerful modern state trying two of its citizens for slander when he said at the trial, "I cannot think that a couple of books by us, or even a score, could inflict substantial damage upon a country like this." And Siniavski remarked in his final plea, "In the whole history of literature I know of no trial like this one." The fact that the writers refused to plead guilty forced the regime to present its flimsy case against them for the world to behold. The leadership, having apparently given them up as sacrificial lambs to the conservative camp and the KGB, looked on silently as Siniav-

[11] Cf. *On Trial.* . . .

ski was sentenced to seven years and Daniel to five years in a labor camp.[12]

It would be impossible to overstate the impact of the Siniavski-Daniel case on the Soviet intellectual community. The conservatives, not surprisingly, felt emboldened and vindicated, and their periodicals, *Oktiabr, Molodaia gvardiia* and *Neva,* carried signed articles duly condemning Siniavski and Daniel. The conservative chief of the Moscow Writers' Union, S. Mikhalkov, also lent his name to a pre-trial castigation of the two men in *Partinaia zhizn.* But the vast majority of Soviet writers and intellectuals, however they may have felt about the indiscretions and writings of the two imprisoned writers, were pained and disturbed by the trial and its implications for Soviet intellectual life. Some maintained an embarrassed silence. But in a show of strength almost unprecedented in the politics of Soviet culture, liberal intellectuals from widely differing professions—scientists, scholars and cultural figures—addressed letters to the party leadership protesting the treatment of the writers and expressing concern over the possible rehabilitation of Stalin and Stalinist policies. The texts of many of these protest notes were later smuggled to the West for publication.[13] The only really major Soviet writer to support the trial publicly was the recent Nobel Prize Winner, Mikhail Sholokhov, who earned the contempt of many of his colleagues by suggesting at the Twenty-third CPSU Congress (two months after the trial) that the sentences were not nearly harsh enough: for this act, one Soviet writer said, "literature has condemned Sholokhov to creative sterility." [14]

The sensational stir created by the Siniavski-Daniel case partially obscured the importance of concurrent developments on the Soviet scene which, it has since become clear, marked the emergence of a new and distinct phase in Soviet cultural policy dating from mid-1965 through 1967. In reviewing these developments, it

[12] One macabre note was added to the affair when the pathologically anti-Soviet writer Valery Tarsis was allowed to go abroad on the eve of the trial and was subsequently deprived of his Soviet citizenship by the authorities.

[13] Cf. *Grani,* November, 1966.

[14] See the amazing letter of Lidiya Chukovskaia to Sholokhov, printed in *The New York Times,* November 19, 1966.

seems simplest to trace two parallel yet, in part at least, contradictory trends that reveal significant ambivalence in the attitude of the leadership. On the one hand, a period of reaction set in that was marked by a number of repressions as harsh, if not as well publicized, as the trial of the two writers, and by a general effort of the regime to reassert discipline and respect for authority—most notably party and police authority—in the society at large. On the other hand, the top leaders persisted in striking an official stance that bespoke a middle of the road outlook on culture, and took pains to demonstrate their support of the "trusted" intelligentsia (including liberals who stayed in line).

The conservative resurgence expressed itself with increasing insistence throughout the fall of 1965 and into the winter. Mounting criticism of the liberal writers was accompanied by loud demands for a more "objective" portrayal of the Stalin era. Military leaders entered actively into the intellectual tug-of-war, blaming the low state of discipline in the armed forces on the prevalence of ideologically impure literature and art. Marshal Krylov (in *Sovetskaia Rossiia* of October 8) laid out an elaborate program for the indoctrination of youth, much in the vein of Pavlov's August outline in *Pravda*. In December Pavlov again made headlines by unleashing a violent diatribe against *Yunost* and announcing further plans for *Komsomol* paramilitary activities. And at the turn of the year a curfew was imposed on young people in Moscow.

Meantime reports began to leak out of a number of repressive actions taken against intellectuals, mainly involving young dissidents. As the poet Yesenin-Volpin is reported to have said, Siniavski and Daniel were lucky in that "their case was taken up by the whole civilized world. There were so many others about whom the . . . world knew nothing—knew as little as people know of a rabbit eaten by the wolves in the forest." [15] To cite some examples that have been reliably reported, the authorities tried to dissipate the *Smogisti* group of young poets after they helped to organize the aforementioned demonstration of December 5, and the KGB actually had one of their leaders, Vladimir Bukovski, interned in an

[15] *The New York Times,* February 20, 1966.

insane asylum as an "invalid of the second category" (a euphe-
mism for a political nonconformist) for six months or more in
1966. At least two other *Smogisti* were arrested but later released.[16] A group of young Leningrad students who had published
an illegal journal called *Kolokol* were arrested and their leaders
sentenced to jail in the fall of 1965.[17] In Moscow several other
young students were arrested, and at least one reportedly sent to
prison, when the police discovered their plan to hold an anti-Stalin
demonstration in Red Square on March 5, 1966, the thirteenth
anniversary of Stalin's death.

The worst repression took place in the Ukraine. Beginning in
the late summer of 1965, as many as seventy Ukrainian intellectuals were reportedly arrested in Kiev, Lvov, Ivano-Franko and
several other cities. Some of those seized were subsequently released, but many were put on trial in the first months of 1966.
According to reports at least twenty were sentenced to two to five
years in labor camps for disseminating and presumably writing
anti-Soviet propaganda.[18] Some verification of these actions has
come from the Soviets. In December, 1965, a spate of articles in
the Soviet press reported on the problem of nationalist activities
among Ukrainian intellectuals. And in the fall of 1966, a young
Ukrainian poet, Ivan Drach, who was visiting the United States,

[16] See dispatch from Moscow in *The Daily Mail* (London), December
17, 1965.
[17] See *Le Figaro* (Paris), January 4, 1966. The circulation of unpublished
manuscripts is extensively practiced among all levels of the intelligentsia,
and many of the best works of recognized Soviet writers are only known
through the "underground." In recent years a few brave souls have ventured
to compile literary anthologies and journals and to send them abroad for
publication. Examples are *Boomerang* (1959), *Lantern* (1965), *Sphinx* and
some of the recent *Smog* collections. The editors of two such journals,
Aleksandr Ginsburg (*Sintaksis*, 1960) and the poet Yuri Galanskov (*Phoenix*,
1961) served prison terms for their activity but afterward continued to
flaunt the authorities. Ginsburg has been identified as the compiler of a new
collection of documents on the Siniavski-Daniel trial, soon to be published
as a "White Paper" in *Grani*, while Galanskov managed to smuggle out a
second edition of his journal (*Phoenix*, 1966). Both men were arrested in
1967 and were held pending a trial.
[18] For accounts of the repressions in the Ukraine, see *The New York
Times*, April 17, 1966; *Le Monde* (Paris), November 16, 1966; and Gabriel
Lorince, "Writers in Revolt," *The New Statesman* (London), December 16,
1966.

publicly acknowledged the arrest and sentencing of several Ukrainian writers, adding that the matter was painful for him since several of his friends were involved.[19] While some of the defendants were no doubt carrying on anti-regime or nationalist activities, a number of writers caught in the crackdown appear to have been guilty of nothing more than individualistic literary efforts that were unsavory to the authorities.

The repression against deviant artists and writers was supported by increased coercion in other areas of society. In March, 1966, new laws were introduced imposing harsher restrictions on religious practices, and in subsequent months demonstration trials and press campaigns made it clear that violators of the laws were being rooted out and disciplined. In July, 1966, the central police ministry (the former MVD, now the MOOP [20]) was reestablished and the militia force enlarged in a stepped-up campaign against "hooliganism" and crime. New legislation strengthened the hands of the militiamen and restricted the courts from being too lenient. Kosygin made it clear that the use of force would continue when he said in June: "It would be incorrect to think that since communism will finally lead to the disappearance of state organs of coercion, one need no longer bother about strengthening public order and can weaken the measures of coercion." [21]

The campaign to build up the image of the police revealed the degree to which the "organs of coercion" had been undermined by Khrushchev's efforts to tame and even discredit them. In this respect the leadership's actions, particularly from September, 1965, on, underscored its serious concern over the breakdown of order and discipline in Soviet society during the years of Khrushchev's rule and over the cumulative tendency of his policies to discredit the Party.

[19] Drach made the statement at a poetry gathering on November 11 at the Overseas Press Club in New York City (see news release of November 18, 1966, issued by Prolog Research & Publishing Assn., New York). It is interesting that Drach's first poem to appear in *Novyi mir* ("Ballad of a Bucket," published in April, 1965) had been translated from the Ukrainian by Yuli Daniel.

[20] This ministry has jurisdiction over the regular police, as distinct from the secret police (KGB). For the preceding five years organizations at the republic level had directed the work of the regular police.

[21] *Pravda,* June 19, 1966.

To turn to the parallel course being pursued by the party leadership, throughout the entire period of disciplinary crackdown the top leaders struck a public posture of following a middle of the road policy on culture. They refused to get overtly involved in the liberal-conservative tug-of-war, though it continued almost unabated. Moreover, they seemed to disassociate themselves from the Siniavski-Daniel case as much as possible. Cultural overseer Demichev is even reported to have passed the word that he felt the crude coverage of the case in *Izvestia* was overdone. At the Twenty-third Party Congress in the spring of 1966 First Secretary Brezhnev did refer to the case with a statement that "the Soviet people" would deal with such "renegades" in the manner they deserved. But other speakers seemed to avoid mention of the trial, though some of the conservatives used the Congress as a forum for attack on other liberal writers in the official family and on *Yunost* and *Novyi mir*. In general the Congress seemed to reflect an official effort to avoid opening any more wounds, while at the same time repudiating extremism of any sort. The removal of Tvardovski and Alexei Surkov from the Central Committee and of Kochetov and Prokofiev from the Central Auditing Commission had the effect of rescinding official recognition of the troublesome extremes; coincidentally it lowered the overall representation of the intelligentsia in the top party organs.[22]

Even more interesting was the official treatment of the better known liberal intellectuals, some of whom were the very men who had borne the heaviest fire in the crisis of 1963. In December, 1965, just when the conservative campaign was mounting to full force, Voznesenki, Yevtushenko and Yefim Dorosh were proposed

[22] A cultural sidelight of the Twenty-third CPSU Congress that reveals the party's "two-faced" approach was the closing down of four of the most controversial plays on the Moscow stage for the two weeks that the Congress delegates were in the "big city." The plays were Aksionov's *Always for Sale*, A. Tvardovski's *Tiorkin in the Other World*, Zorin's *Dion*, and E. Radzinski's *Making a Movie*. All the plays deal in some way with the Stalinist heritage and were apparently considered too daring for the provincial delegates and out of tune with the generally conservative tone of the Congress. After the Congress all the plays reopened. (See *The New York Times*, April 20, 1966.) However, *Tiorkin*—the play most critical of Stalinism—did not reappear in the 1966-67 theater season.

as candidates for the Lenin Prize in Literature for some of their most controversial works. During 1966 the regime permitted a number of the liberals to travel abroad; Yevtushenko, Voznesenki and Aksionov each made several trips to various countries, and even Ernst Neizvestny and the ballad-singer, Bulat Okudzhava, were allowed their first foreign junkets. In the same period, the liberal intellectuals were making more frequent appearances before Soviet audiences. No doubt the regime was motivated in part by the desire to counter criticism of the Siniavski-Daniel trial with a demonstration of liberality. For their part, the young liberals—while not fully comfortable in their role as beneficiaries of the repression of the two writers—seemed to recognize the pragmatic need to keep their foot in the door with the Party.

Throughout 1966 and 1967, the pattern of events continued to reflect the two strands of the leadership's stance vis-à-vis the intellectual community. The Party seemed to come to the tentative conclusion that by permitting cultural experimentation and foreign imports—within bounds—the intellectuals' energies could be sidetracked from potentially more dangerous anti-regime activity. At the same time, there was no let up in the authorities' efforts to quell the intellectual underground; indeed, the recent strengthening of laws against anti-Soviet propaganda, as well as continuing reports of arrests among young intellectuals, seemed to reflect the regime's determination to impress upon the intellectual community the lesson that dissidence does not pay. Finally, while the top leadership continued to stand aloof from the conservative-liberal struggle, there were persistent indications that official pressure was being brought to bear in certain ideological "problem areas." For example, the editors of *Yunost*—the *bête noire* of the conservatives—were eventually induced to "confess" their ideological sins, and in the opinion of many observers the magazine's liberal stance thereafter showed signs of dilution; curiously, however, *Yunost* was allowed to raise its circulation to two million a month in 1966. There were also many signs that the authorities were pressing for changes in the editorial board and policies of *Novyi mir*.

The reaction of the liberal intellectuals to these various official policies and pressures was quite different from what it had been in the 1962-63 period of crackdown, when so many of them chose the "conspiracy of silence" as their best means of protest. We have already noted the remarkable strength and unity demonstrated by various segments of the moderate and liberal intelligentsia in protesting the trial of Siniavski and Daniel. Encouraged, perhaps, by this expression of an overwhelming consensus, the liberals did not retreat into silence, but rather sought other more subtle ways, in their writings and in their actions, to keep alive the crucial issues of the "little truth," the artist's freedom, the dangers of persisting Stalinism. The editors of *Novyi mir* continued to assert their independence—and courage—by publishing prose and criticism that expressed the liberal point of view, and *Yunost's* retreat was only marginal.[23] The liberals also kept up their protest against censorship, holding that open criticism of Soviet society not only should be allowed but was essential to its health—as one spokesman put it succinctly, "for Russia, the doctor is publicity [*yasnost*]." [24]

Nor was the intellectual underground much intimidated. No greater act of defiance could have been devised than the smuggling abroad of the Siniavski-Daniel trial record and the protest notes on the case—the very crime for which the two writers had been incarcerated. The extent to which young dissidents and intellectuals remained recalcitrant was revealed by two incidents in Moscow on the same day—January 22, 1967. In Pushkin Square some twenty-five to fifty young people put official tolerance to the test by a demonstration in protest against Article 70 of the Criminal Code—the article under which Siniavski and Daniel had been condemned and under which other writers have since been arrested.[25] Elsewhere in the city, at a trade union club, twelve of Moscow's leading underground painters opened an exhibit of their paintings. The show was closed by the authorities within two hours, but only after over 500 people had managed to see it. Yevtushenko reportedly decried the closing, defended the artists,

---

23 One of the most significant recent pieces in *Yunost* (Nos. 9 and 10, 1966) was Vasili Kuznetsov's *Babi Yar: A Documentary Novel,* an elaboration of the theme of Yevtushenko's famous poem published in 1962.

24 See *Grani,* November, 1966, p. 16.

25 On these arrests, see *The New York Times,* January 24, 1967.

blamed the action on the bureaucrats in the Union of Artists, and suggested, according to one report, that the top party officials might have allowed the show to go on had they not been "too high up to be concerned with things like this." [26]

Yevtushenko's remark reflected the degree to which liberals felt helplessly cut off from the top of the power structure, even as they continued to press for changes in cultural policy. Ironically—if what they wanted was some intervention from on high—they were about to get it. But the word that was issued, presumably with top-level sanction, was hardly what they yearned to hear. On January 27, 1967, an editorial in *Pravda* offered the first extensive policy statement on the arts since the removal of Rumiantsev in September, 1965. The editorial had sharp criticisms for both extremes in the continuing "conservative-liberal" conflict, and was probably aimed at toning down the debate in preparation for the much-postponed Fourth Soviet Union Writers' Congress, as well as for the general celebration of the fiftieth anniversary of the October Revolution. Yet there was no doubt where the most significant criticism fell. In the most explicit terms to date, the editorial spelled out the regime's objection to *Novyi mir's* editorial policies of publishing literature and critical essays that centered on the negative side of Soviet society, that defended "anti-heroes," and that failed to view the fifty years of Soviet history from the standpoint of "universality." The statement was a clear repudiation of the former Rumiantsev line defending the artist's privilege to write his "private truths," demonstrating the degree to which reaction had set in over the preceding months. Though more than token criticism was

[26] Quoted in a dispatch from Moscow to *The Washington Post* (Washington, D.C.), January 27, 1967. Throughout the period of repression against the dissident writers of 1965-66, the underground painters had seemingly been allowed a good deal of freedom to sell their paintings to foreigners and to their patrons among Soviet scientists and "establishment" intellectuals. Two of them (Oskar Rabin and Anatoli Zverev) had even managed to sneak out paintings and have shows abroad. Rabin was the target of a scurrilous attack in *Sovetskaia kultura* on June 15, 1966, but it did not seem to harm his unofficial standing, and in general the underground market continued to flourish. The January 22 exhibit showed fifty abstract and expressionist canvases by Rabin, Zverev, Plavinski, Nemukhin, Masterkova, Kropovnitski—the older and the younger—and five other artists.

directed at *Oktiabr*—for holding itself up as the only authority on
"Socialist Realism," for producing "grey" literature, and for not
accepting de-Stalinization—this was little compensation to the
elements in Soviet society who looked to *Novyi mir* as the con-
science of the Soviet intellectual and the only real defender of the
Russian literary tradition.

The editorial in *Pravda* marked the most definitive indication of
the current trend of Soviet cultural policy as of this writing. It is
time, then, to look backward over the 1965-1967 period, to recognize that what has transpired on the cultural front is only part
of the broad spectrum of what has been going on in the Soviet
world, and to try to relate the cultural scene to the overall impera-
tives of leadership policy.

The developments in Soviet culture since the ouster of Khrushchev demonstrate what was already known—that the intellectual
currents in Soviet society are intertwined with the politics and
policies of the party leadership in complex and confusing ways.
The sequence of events described above does, however, suggest
some observations on the manner in which the Brezhnev-Kosygin
leadership has evolved.

First, it seems clear that the changes on the cultural front in the
summer and early fall of 1965 reflected the resolution within the
party of broader political issues and most probably stemmed from
a realignment within the top leadership. By September, Party First
Secretary Brezhnev seems to have reconciled to his advantage the
disparate forces at work over the preceding ten months. A number
of factors point to the conclusion that August-September of 1965
was a watershed in the leadership's programs and policies, and in
the career of Brezhnev: (1) Rumiantsev's removal in September
as editor of *Pravda* marked the end of that paper's short-lived
practice of taking polemical and relatively "liberal" stances on key
policy issues, suggesting strongly that he had been replaced in a
policy controversy; (2) within a few months after September,
most of the major central newspapers and political journals were
assigned new editors-in-chief, and important new assignments were
made to the ideological and propaganda branches of the Party and
government, indicating that a new first team was being installed

with new instructions; (3) Nikolai Podgorny, who had been one of Brezhnev's chief rivals under Khrushchev, was "kicked upstairs" in December, 1965, to become titular chief of state; Podgorny had appeared on at least one occasion in the spring of 1965 as a chief spokesman for moderate policies in the economy, and his prior association with Rumiantsev allows speculation that he may have influenced Rumiantsev's appointment to *Pravda* immediately after Khrushchev's ouster; (4) Party Secretary Shelepin, who reportedly planned or made a move for more power some time in the latter half of 1965, was trimmed back in December, 1965, when he was relieved of the party-state control apparatus. (5) after the fall of 1965 virtually every major appointment to the government or Party was either a man long associated with Brezhnev or a figure representing Brezhnev's particular bias for older party leaders from the provinces. One seeming inconsistency in this picture is that many of the new appointments in the cultural and propaganda sector seemed to come from the younger party cadres, suggesting that in the September "reconciliation," the younger Politiburo members, perhaps represented by Shelepin, Mazurov and Demichev, were given an important voice in policies and personnel assignments in the field of ideology and culture.

The policy lines that emerged after September, 1965, reflected on one hand the Party's heightened awareness of the nation's economic ills and its preparedness to make some innovations to meet them, and on the other hand the Party's proclivity in the social and political sectors to resort to old formulas.[27] What has emerged over the 1965-1967 period, then, has been a peculiar combination of programs for reform and retrenchment, relaxation and discipline: (1) the economic measures adopted at the crucial September, 1965, Central Committee plenum were a moderate but important step toward reform of the economy—although the recentrali-

[27] The intensified conflict in Southeast Asia and the heightened Sino-Soviet dispute most certainly gave added weight to the arguments of those who in the fall of 1965 were pressing for more ideological orthodoxy and vigilance at home and less emphasis on exchanges with the West. In relations with the Chinese, there was also a noticeable sharpening of the debate within the movement from the Soviet side in the fall of 1965, culminating in the December Soviet letter to all Communist parties.

zation of the government and economic administration seemed to vitiate many of the reformist aspects; (2) Party officials were warned not to meddle too deeply in the economy—yet the changes made in the party structure and style were orthodox and fundamentalist; (3) in the face of evident opposition, particularly from the intelligentsia, the Party was forced to slow down its campaign to rehabilitate the Stalin era—but increasing stress was put on refurbishing the image of the Party, the heroic past and the police; (4) new stress was placed on sociological and scientific work to determine public needs—yet in the much debated area of legal reforms and "guarantees," in the face of a continued high incidence of crime, there seemed to be a regression to greater use of repressive organs; (5) the scientific establishment was restructured to encourage technological progress, and more latitude seemed to be granted cultural figures for experimentation—yet in the field of thought and expression in general, violators of official controls were severely punished in evident efforts to impose discipline by example, and censorship was tightened on writing critical of the Party and police in the Stalin era.

The conclusion seems to be that Brezhnev patched together a conservative leadership bent on restoring the Party's prestige but also seriously interested in improving the efficiency of the economy. In the deal, the moderate or "liberal conservative" line of Rumiantsev was moved out of the propaganda sector—but it has not been wholly abandoned. Rumiantsev himself has remained active in setting up the new work on sociology, and the policies he espoused still seem to be the unspoken rationale behind the official encouragement given to some segments of the intelligentsia. While the "hardliners" seem to have the upper hand in the Brezhnev coalition on matters of "legality" and discipline, it is unlikely that the leadership is prepared to introduce extreme enough methods of control and repression to retard significantly the breakdown in the authority and ideology of the Party. Therefore, the "liberal conservatives" in the Party are relied upon to seek out more subtle methods to tame the youth, channel their intellectual vigor, and—insofar as possible—reinforce their patriotism.

There seems to be little hope that the Brezhnev leadership as it is now constituted will ever allow a major relaxation of controls over the intellectuals. The provincial Party, and the military and police lobbies have too strong a voice in the Brezhnev collective leadership and in any foreseeable coalitions to allow hope that the "liberal conservative" element will gain dominance in the cultural field. At the same time—barring the unlikely return to extreme repression—the gains in the expansion of culture over recent years will not be undone, and the various intellectual forces in the Soviet Union can be expected to continue pressing forward with marginal moves to open up the society.

Brezhnev, however, is still faced with the same dilemma Khrushchev had—how to adapt the Party to its leadership role and keep its ideology relevant to Soviet society and the Communist movement. For a short period in 1965, when the leaders were most unsure of their directions, they seemed cautiously to seek the assistance of the intellectuals in taking some moderate steps toward adapting the Soviet establishment to modern needs. However "scientific" their orientation has been since that time, the leaders have demonstrated that the Party's bias remains anti-intellectual, resistant to change, and distrustful of the artist. One Soviet intellectual who lived through both 1953-54 and 1964-65 "thaws," and who understood clearly this persistent inflexibility of the party leadership, has suggested that what the Soviet Union obviously needs is frequent leadership changes, so that during the confusing interregna, the management of the country can be left to those who know what must be done and the intellectuals can benefit from the relative freedom that flows from disorientation at the top.

## A Digression on Labels

Writers and artists in the Soviet Union, in one sense, are more *engagés* in the world in which they live than are their Western contemporaries. Since, as critics, reformers, caricaturists or defenders of the status quo, they cannot participate directly in a democratic political process, their works take on a particular urgency and become the focus of their political involvement. In describing the activities of the intellectuals, analysts have found it convenient over the years to speak of "liberals" and "conservatives" in depicting the two poles of the intensely political Soviet culture. By "liberals" we mean those intellectuals who are dedicated to increased candor and truth, relaxation of controls, greater personal freedom, and the complete eradication of the Stalinist heritage. In contrast, the "conservatives" are understood to be those who demand the retention of orthodoxy in order to preserve the existing order; for them, criticism of the Stalin era is unpatriotic and detracts from the revolutionary goals of Soviet society.

Yet the terms "liberal" and "conservative" do not adequately describe the multiversity of artistic commitments in the Soviet Union today, and their implications for Western readers may tend to oversimplify the tangled web of the politics of Soviet culture. Many of the political "liberals" are—in matters of culture—conservative, in the sense that they are deeply attached to the Russian past. Conversely, many "conservatives" eschew all ties with pre-Stalin Russia. Thus it is necessary to break down the liberal-to-conservative spectrum into other groupings based largely on attitudes toward art and culture, realizing that no work of art—nor artist—can be considered totally apolitical in the Soviet state. Below I have identified and labeled several such elements. I do not mean to suggest that these arbitrary labels describe formal groupings within the intelligentsia or encompass by any means all the variety in Soviet culture. They have been chosen simply as a framework within which to discuss the growing diversity of the cultural scene and to point up the confusing problems this pluralism presents to the Party.

The political reactionaries who dominate *Oktiabr,* the Academy of Fine Arts, the RSFSR Writers' organization, and the Unions of Composers and Artists are essentially unreconstructed Stalinists whose superpatriotism and inferior esthetic taste are anathema to the vast majority of Soviet intellectuals, and often an embarrassment to the Party, particularly to its younger members. Generally from the older generation, the "dogmatists" are obsessed with maintaining restrictions over form, unwilling to experiment with new artistic genres, fearful of losing their privileges and patronage rights in Soviet society, and most adamant in their opposition to cultural exchange with the West. Despite their apparently hegemonic position in their own organizations, they have on occasion been forced to modify their stand by progressive elements in the *Komsomol,* the government and even the Party.

The "slavophiles" are composed generally of the self-consciously Russian intellectuals, who are fascinated by the symbols of pre-Petrine Russia and the Orthodox church. Mainly from the younger generation, they seek identity with the slavophile writers and artists of the nineteenth century and tend to denigrate foreign influences and intrusions on "pure" Russian art. Official writers and artists rarely espouse these ideas publicly, but "slavophilism" pervades the ideas and works of many dissident poets and painters who work outside the establishment. Certain elements in the *Komsomol,* including on occasion the noted cultural heavyweight, Sergei Pavlov, have sought to capitalize on this widespread enthusiasm and curiosity about the Russian past as a means of countering the impact of Western thought, and stimulating patriotism. The *Komsomol* literary journal, *Molodaia gvardiia,* for example, has published extensive "slavophile" journals by the painter Ilia Glazunov and the writer Vladimir Soloukhin, and the *Komsomols* in 1965 organized *Rodina* (motherland) clubs to study prerevolutionary Russian culture.

Probably the most talented group in the cultural spectrum, the "Russian traditionalists," most closely resemble the traditional Russian *intelligent.* Firmly committed to restoring vitality and spirit-

uality to Russian culture, they have little interest in Western political concepts. They differ from the slavophiles in that they are more
mature, less chauvinistic with respect to non-Russian influences,
and considerably more committed to the eradication of Stalinist
blights. Like the slavophiles, however, they are attracted by the
symbols of "eternal Russia," chiefly the Orthodox church and the
Russian village. Aleksandr Tvardovski, the able editor of the "liberal" stronghold, *Novyi mir,* can probably be considered the chief
sponsor of this group. He has published the works of such noted
writers as Solzhenitsyn, Mozhaev, Tendriakov, Semin, Yashin,
Abramov, Kazakov, none of whom could be considered liberals in
the Western sense, but who seem to represent the "Russian tradi-
tionalist" point of view. Andrei Siniavski, whose strong individu-
ality confounds all labels, might nevertheless be considered a
member of this group. He has been characterized a "slavophile" in
the philosophical sense of the term, and he has taken a forceful
"liberal" position in the struggle against all that is philistine, dogmatic and Stalinist in Soviet society. Yet his critique of the Soviet
system and of Socialist Realism in particular is based essentially
on Russian conservative values and emotional entrancement with
Russian culture and history, so much so that his decision to send
his manuscripts to the West might well have confounded many of
his admirers among the "slavophiles" or the "traditionalists." Western liberals, on the other hand, have not been able to understand
his conservatism on some issues, specifically his refusal to condemn
unqualifiedly the Stalin era during his trial. Rationalizing Stalinist
brutalities, Siniavski explained that they resulted from action
against inertia. His reply to liberal critics was: "And what have all
you humane dodderers achieved?"

The "liberal conservatives" are composed of men and women who
have emerged from the Khrushchev era fully accepting de-Stalinization but too ensconced in the establishment and/or too involved
personally in the Stalin era to take a lead in pressing for further
revelations of the past. The group includes representatives from all
generations who share the belief that the Party and the intellectuals
must work hand in hand toward a moderate change in Soviet society. They presumably see Soviet cultural life gradually playing a

larger role in Western culture while retaining its ideological and patriotic flavor. In the Party this view was expressed by Alexei Rumiantsev, while in the cultural community it seems best represented by such reconstructed Stalinists as Alexei Surkov and Konstantin Simonov, as well as younger writers like Yuri Bondariov and Robert Rozhdestvenski. With supporters in the Moscow and Leningrad writers' organizations, and in government organs such as the Ministry of Culture, the "liberal conservatives" have been influential in enlarging the variety and improving the quality of foreign literature available in Russian and have played an important role in promoting cultural exchanges.

Through artistic style and bold behavior, the "modern liberals" have introduced a new vitality into Soviet cultural life. This group is composed primarily of writers and artists in their thirties or early forties, including Bella Akhmadulina, Yuri Nagibin, Andrei Voznesenski, Vasili Aksionov, Bulat Okudzhava, Aleksandr Volodin, Anatoli Gladilin, Viktor Nekrasov, Vladimir Maximov, Yevgeni Yevtushenko, the sculptor Ernst Neizvestny and the composer Andrei Volkonski. The group enjoys the support of many notable members of the older generation—*e.g.,* Ilya Ehrenburg, Viktor Rozov, Valentin Kataev, Kornei Chukovski and Mikhail Romm. Centered around the magazine *Yunost* and such theaters as the Sovremennik and "Taganka" in Moscow and the Gorky in Leningrad, this group has been producing literary and artistic works which, for Soviet conditions, are refreshingly new and sophisticated. Broadly speaking, the aim of these writers and artists is to forge a link between a modernized, multinational Soviet culture and the culture of the contemporary West. They have consistently sought contacts with American and European intellectuals. Supported by influential members of the scientific and academic communities, they have also been increasingly open in carrying their cause to the party leadership.

As has been suggested, each of these groups presents its own set of dilemmas for the party leadership, for while they may all be useful at one time or another, none of them can be counted on to follow the inconsistent party line consistently. The "dogmatists" offer needed support for certain ideological and propaganda goals, but they are often a hindrance to the Party in its efforts to win the good will of the larger intellectual community at home or abroad. The "slavophiles" are useful to the regime in countering Western cultural influence and in stimulating Russian patriotism, but their arguments have nothing to do with Marxism-Leninism; in fact, their emphasis on purely Russian culture, their disparagement of other national cultures, and their often implicit anti-Semitism offend the sensibilities of other Soviet nationalities. The "Russian traditionalists" pose the most serious dilemma for the Party. Clearly among the most  talented and influential of Soviet artists and writers, they have been the most incisive in their attacks on the Stalinist past and the most effective in their portrayal of the seamier sides of Soviet life today. The "liberal conservatives," while most attuned to the policy of the progressives in the Party, have been a constant source of irritation to the provincial Party, police and military establishments, all of which view with alarm any signs of tolerance toward Western cultural and political values. A similar duality may also be observed in the Party's attitude towards the "modern liberals." On one hand, they have proved to be effective "unofficial diplomats" at home and abroad, probably doing more to generate goodwill and sympathy for the Soviet Union than all the official professions of "peaceful coexistence" combined. Yet the "modern liberals" have also been most persistently in the forefront of the struggle against such ugly manifestations of Stalinist mentality as xenophobia and anti-Semitism.

In conclusion, one caveat is in order: whatever the challenges of the above outlined groups to the regime, their basic loyalty is not to be questioned. Each is patriotic in its own way and on its own terms, and few Soviet intellectuals would, if given an opportunity, follow in the footsteps of Tarsis. But the Party is not always cognizant of the distinction between "loyal opposition" and political disloyalty. As some of its repressive measures in the recent past have indicated, it is also afraid lest the ferment of the creative intelligentsia vitiate its effort to restore some vigor to a state ideology. These apprehensions are not unreasonable: the ferment *is* contagious, and the pretensions of the official ideology are viewed with growing skepticism by an increasingly sophisticated public.

Contributing to this erosion of dogma, too, are the activities of the "underground" writers and artists and the apparently "fearless" intellectuals of the new generation, whose impatience with the reformist proclivities of the "official intelligentsia" shows no signs of diminishing. Given all these conflicting trends, one conjecture may be safely essayed: the Soviet cultural scene will continue to be rife with tensions and proverbial "internal contradictions" for years to come.

# 8

---

## A Decade of Significance for Religion: 1956-1966

### PAUL B. ANDERSON

DURING THE middle period of Soviet rule in the Soviet Union, the Party made an attempt to correlate its anti-religious program with the economic program of the several Five-Year Plans. The harsh methods used in collectivization and in the high-speed industrialization of the country were similarly applied to religion, but in this case aimed at destruction rather than construction. Externally great success was achieved, for church central offices and local places of worship, both Orthodox and other, were crushed and reduced to fragments. Islam suffered the same fate.

An upturn came, however, with the Second World War, when the need for national unity in Russia overcame atheistic zeal; the militant godless society was disbanded; the participation of church leaders and of the faithful generally was welcomed instead of shunned; and there seemed to be signs of a restoration of Holy Russia. As the Nazi armies were thrown back and as the Soviet Union extended its frontier westward, religious life rebounded as with the release of a spring. Thousands of churches which had been functioning in the territory under Polish rule, or under the occupation forces of the Nazi armies in the Ukraine, now came within the extended limits of the Soviet empire. For several years they were permitted to exist. These newly acquired churches, to-

---

Paul B. Anderson is a consultant to the National Council of Churches in New York.

gether with some thousands of reopened churches in Russia itself, brought the total up to the 20,000 reported by the Moscow Patriarchate in its 1959 application for membership in the World Council of Churches.

All of this took place under Stalin. His regime continued for eight years after the war, up to March, 1953. These years can be accounted favorable for the Orthodox and the Baptists, but, paradoxically, unfavorable for the Catholics and the Jews. In 1946 came the great loss to the Catholic church of the Byzantine rite Catholics, the Uniats, who "returned" to the bosom and administration of the Russian Orthodox church. This was a result of the Soviet government's policy of requiring maximum unity in church organization. The Orthodox church had its own motivation for cooperation in this policy, based on the claim that in 1596 the Vatican had forcibly withdrawn the faithful Orthodox in this region by applying the Union of Florence of 1439 to the Brest and Wolhynia provinces of Poland, thus placing hundreds of thousands of Orthodox under Catholic bishops and papal authority. It is estimated that some 3,500,000 Uniats "returned" in 1946. This chapter will deal later with the present position of these people and of the Latin Rite Catholics in the Soviet Union.

As regards the Jews, attention need only be called to two events which had an adverse effect on the practice of the Jewish religion in Russia. The first was the establishment of the state of Israel in 1948. As an act of national liberation, this was welcomed by the Soviets; but as an expression of Zionism, a Jewish homeland, with an appeal to all Jews everywhere, it created the threat of a rise of double loyalty among Jews in Russia. This contradicted the Soviet's demand for exclusive and complete loyalty. The second thing that hurt the Jews was the so-called "doctors' plot" against Stalin. However false the accusations, the effect was to stir up the endemic anti-Semitism of the public. As a result of these and other factors, the Jewish religious communities in Russia have been deprived of the right of having a national organization, of theological education and of traditional items needed for worship, especially at festival time.

So much for the Stalin period. Twenty months after his death, the Party issued a decree, dated November 10, 1954, signed by

Nikita Khrushchev, which apparently was intended to be a statement of new policy, but which actually was a rehash of state legislation and party policy developed since Lenin's time, including the oft-repeated and constantly broken rule, to avoid offense to believers. Some interpreted this decree as a new and favorable sign; others as one foreboding ill. As a matter of fact, it was not until five years later that a decisive event occurred which had a definitive negative effect on religion in the Soviet Union. This event was the convening of a national conference on ideological problems, and its acceptance of a harsh line, as set forth in a report by the head of the Party's ideological commission, Ilichev. While the meeting itself was not publicized, the Ilichev document was given a prominent place in the big dailies and journals, and from it there sprang a whole series of measures aimed at the suffocation of the Church and the eventual eradication of religion. On this also more detail will be given later in this chapter.

Up to this point we have followed the usual practice of dealing with religion in Russia in terms of relationships between churches and the government. For many years, in fact until 1960, there was not much else to write about, as little information was available on the internal life of religious bodies, on the thinking of religious persons, whether on theology or on secular matters, or on the trends within the Party toward a fresh examination of its stand on religion. Now we have the advantage of a large amount of published and unpublished Soviet material dealing with the ideas of people in the churches and with the *aggiornamento* of the Party's philosophy on religion. This information comes largely in articles in the "big" journals such as *Questions of Philosophy, Kommunist, Political Self-Education,* and in a deluge of large and small volumes published by government presses. The two chief religious journals, the one published by the Patriarchate and the other by the All-Union Council of Evangelical Christians-Baptists, have become increasingly descriptive instead of being dryly official.

The Soviet press has published a number of reports on sociological-religious surveys conducted by teams sent out by the Academy of Science, by a university, or by some other state agency. Each survey deals with a specified territory, which may be as large as a province (*oblast*) or as small as a single *kolkhoz*. There seems to be no uniformity in the methodology, and so far no attempt at achieving a composite, comprehensive, nationwide picture. In a way this diversity and scattering of surveys is good because, despite improved transportation and communications systems, the various parts of the vast territory of the Soviet Union are too diversified in language, religion and customs to lend themselves to a single pattern of study covering all religions and places.

In addition to these valuable, detailed scientific reports, prepared, to be sure, by single-minded atheists, a number of documents prepared by religious people themselves have made their way to the West, of which none has been published in the Soviet Union. However, when a document is adequately authenticated, it can be used as source material. First to arrive were "protest" or "appeal" documents, chiefly from rural areas, as far apart as the Western Ukraine and the Altai mountains of Siberia, mostly written in rather uncultured language. Subsequently copies of formal documents addressed to the government, to the Patriarchate, or to the Baptist headquarters were received. Some of these are well-constructed in thought and style. In 1966 came some which are based on the canons and theology of the Orthodox church, and reveal a fine sense of the reality of religious experience under Soviet conditions. Some of these documents have been referred to but not published in the Soviet secular press. In addition, a good deal is learned about individuals, groups and districts from news items in the Soviet central and provincial papers, and especially from articles in the Russian and Ukrainian anti-religious journals. Even law journals are helpful, as they interpret old and new legislation on religion, and comment on court procedures at trials where religious people have been indicted and sentenced by the magistrates. Finally, poetry, novels, short stories and essays in the literary magazines may be mentioned; these may not be "real", but they portray the attitudes of people as the authors sense them, and they reflect life as it is.

What can be harvested from this rich field of information, so much in contrast with the sources of a decade ago? The chief impression one gets is that religion, while retaining its structure and regaining the interest of the intelligentsia, is suffering a severe decline in the great body of Soviet citizens. During the centuries the religiosity of the Russian people has gone through periods of rise and fall. If we take only the Soviet era, the crest seems to have come during the Second World War, followed by a slow decline for about five years, then a more precipitous drop for three or four years, with a trough established at about 1965. It would not be fair to charge state or party anti-religious policy with full responsibility for the losses sustained, whether in terms of the number of faithful, or in closed churches, or in the content of belief. Much of this has come about as a result of the impact of social and economic factors, not the least being the weight of fifty years of the heavy atmosphere of party domination, with its powerful demand for change. Communism means change.

Thus, collectivization not only changed the form of land tenure and its cultivation, it uprooted the traditional religious calendar for sowing and reaping, and got the people to depend on agricultural science rather than divine favor for the harvest. The closing of village churches was not always a violent act of godless bureaucrats; many times the people simply failed to attend services in sufficient number to meet the financial obligations of the contract with the State for maintenance, repair and insurance on the church building. This was particularly true of the churches recovered from Nazi occupation in southwestern Russia, where many churches closed by the godless movement in the nineteen-thirties had been reopened in the first flush of release from Communist domination, as we have described earlier.

Industrialization was an even more important enemy of religion. Again, it was a matter of filling people's minds and occupying their time with other things, to the exclusion of attention to God. The forced movement of large segments of the population from their ancestral homes to the far corners of the Soviet Union, usually to new industrial centers where there were no churches and where facilities for building them were denied, left great numbers unchurched and without pastors—Orthodox, Catholic or Protestant.

Most important of all, of course, has been the education of children in schools where religion is not only absent but is denied and attacked. If we are to judge by examination of textbooks and by educational and teachers' journals, the atheistic content of curricula in the lower schools is not uniform. Not every subject lends itself to either the advocating or the attacking of religion. Much depends on the mood and intent of the teacher, who in turn is influenced by personal conviction and, to some extent, by school administrative officers and especially by the ubiquitous ideological agitators maintained by the Communist party. At the same time, one is occasionally struck at finding not merely a neutral but a positively religious tone among teachers and pupils in some schools. The secular press reports that in some places boys and girls enter churches at odd hours to place their candles and to say a prayer, especially at examination time.

Education, however takes place not only in the classroom but at work and play. Most of the children are drawn into the "October" or "Pioneer" groups, whose adult leaders are quite strictly screened and trained to ensure atheistic leanings. These Communist movements for children are on the whole exceedingly well-handled, providing nearly full occupation of hours not required in school or for preparation of lessons at home. Play, excursions, games, hobbies, children's theaters, self-expression of all forms— these are the effective means used to nurture Soviet children in the spirit and fill them with the content of Communist party goals. These principles are built upon and enforced in the *Komsomol,* but youth of this age—eighteen to twenty-six—are less amenable to the restrictions; doubts are formed; some of which are resolved on religious lines.

When a Soviet boy or girl enters a technical school or the university, the chances are that religion plays little or no part in his life. Nevertheless, occasionally there appears striking evidence of deeply submerged religiosity, completely undiscernible to other students or to professors, but brought to the surface by some chance incident leading to awareness of common religious feeling with another student. All of this is discreetly handled, for self-protection, as the record of expulsion for religious belief is high.

There are of course thousands, indeed millions of youths who do not enroll in higher educational institutions. Are they free of the restraints and pressures which face the college student? Atheism is of the essence of Soviet society, or at least it is supposed to be. The young man who enters military service is put through an even tougher course of atheism than he would have had at college, and the girl who stays on the collective farm or who works in a factory or office comes under the scrutiny of the personnel official charged by the Party with detecting any evidence of religiosity in the plant. Here again practice is highly varied. Time and again the Soviet press reports on religious persons who are "among our best workers." But almost as often such a report is followed some days later with another, which tells of success in "liberating" the worker from religious captivity, or of his discharge. This is accomplished by what might be called personal evangelism in reverse. There are still many cases of violence against religious persons, as will be described later, but the preferred and characteristic method of fighting religion during the present decade is by the person-to-person method. It must be remembered that the Party has long been conducting special schools and short-term institutes for the training of anti-religious workers, with the result that tens of thousands have now been carefully instructed on the method and content of anti-religious work. Such a worker must study the history, the sacred books and the psychology of religion. His approach is now less frequently that of a lecture, but more likely a friendly conversation on a subject of common interest, say fertilizer or factory output, followed by a visit with the family, noting but not criticizing ikons or other evidences of religion in the home. Judging by success stories in the anti-religious journals, the agitator may need to use patience and skill for weeks before the "eyes are opened," and the darkness of religious faith is removed.

Back of all of these methods, restraints, pressures and incentives there lies a dominant factor, which was explained to the writer some years ago by a priest in a small town near the Polish border. He said that hitherto the peasants or the artisans had simply been doing what their fathers had done, counting on the mercy of God to provide a living, even though a hard one; they would grow old; they would expect to die, and the Church would lay them to rest. Now, said the priest, all is different. The county agent has come and showed how chemical fertilizer will increase the crop; the artisan is invited to a factory where he earns good wages. Thanks to these changes, the lure of gain had supplanted faith in God's providence.

The more sophisticated methods used in combatting religion are, in a way, a reflection of the claim of Marxism-Leninism to be scientific. Prejudice and subjectivism must give way to knowledge and objectivity. It is interesting to note that Vol. 56 of Lenin's collected works, issued in 1956, publishes for the first time Lenin's handwritten marginal comment on a 1921 decree drafted by Lunacharsky on the matter of religion. Lenin instructs that the decree be reviewed by Jaroslavsky and Bukharin, and that the revision provide against giving offense to believers. It was so revised, but how little heed has been given to this instruction! The Party and the authorities at all levels have struck at religion by crudely handling or even physically destroying the believer.

In the nineteen-sixties this continues, but the foundations for a more objective and humane approach to believers and churches are being laid by sociological surveys and psychological studies in the field of religion. Thus the Academy of Science in 1959-60 sponsored a sociological survey of religious sectarians in the Tambov region, one of the surveyors being L. N. Mitrokhin, a very able and kindly person who has twice been in the United States with exchange groups. Other studies have covered the Lutherans and the Old Believers in Latvia, the Orthodox in a restricted locality in Byelorussia, the Roman Catholics in Lithuania, and others. Here is a paragraph regarding such a study:

> It is necessary to know, firstly, the extent and character of religiosity of the population in the given locality: how many, age, and educational level of believers, the type of their work, their confessional adherence, the depth of their religious feelings, the reason for their religiousness, etc.; secondly, the methods used by the ministers of religion and laity to exercise influence on believers and on the public generally.[1]

In Byelorussia the survey examined 7,000 adults and 2,000 schoolchildren. "Conversations with believers established: the rites they observed, frequency and reasons for church attendance, what attracts them there, fasting and what they know about religious festivals, their image of God and of the saints, belief in life

[1] *Problems of Overcoming Religious Vestiges in the USSR,* Academy of Science, Moscow, 1966.

beyond the grave, in hell and in paradise, in supernatural powers, when and what led to belief in the existence of God (was it family, neighbors, relatives, workers in the church or sect), their attitude toward scientific achievements, space travel." [2]

In the Ukraine a study of fifty to eighty persons was made in each of several parishes. The Tambov survey by the Academy of Science was conducted by a team consisting of three historians, three ethnographers and one philosopher, with the help of local workers. Special study was made of the sect called "True Ortho-dox Christians" (a breakaway from the Patriarchate), based on detailed recordings of conversations with collective farm workers, employees, village intelligentsia, local party and soviet workers, true Orthodox Christians and Orthodox believers. They gathered material on ideology, faith and hymns, and on the activities of the anti-religious workers. The findings of the study were published in a rather large book complete with tables.

An interesting case is that of the study in five districts in and around Gatchina in Leningrad province. This was undertaken when it was discovered that the Party was conducting no anti-religious work there because "there was only one church with a few old women." More than 500 families were visited, and the results enabled the Party to vitalize its anti-religious work.

Another study covered the atheist workers themselves in three large towns. Although "only nineteen percent of the question-naires were filled out," the study led to important observations. "One-fifth of the replies said that the chief means for strengthening work against religion was the closing of churches, and most of them did no individual work with believers." One of the surveys purposely covered seventy-seven families in a collective farm where all churches had long been closed. On the other hand, they had a school, hospital, library, clubs; all have radios and some have television. The study showed that religion is still active: many have ikons; celebrate religious holidays; baptize their children; and without religious fanaticism hold to strong traditions.

Here are a few additional observations from the reports of the survey teams. The reason for turning to religion is chiefly "the hard life." The intensity of religious life rises and fades. Effective

[2] *Ibid.*

atheistic work requires data on age, sex, education and place of work. Putting together the results of many surveys in various parts of the Soviet Union, it was found that "the great majority of believers are women, older persons and persons not engaged in productive work; most of them having very little education and low occupational skill." While "some comrades" tend to look upon believers as enemies, a study in Penza showed that "almost all see the purpose in life as being the construction of communism."

The modern approach is not content with surveys of individuals; it embraces also study of "church manuscripts and printed literature, documents regarding church activity, observations during services in churches and monasteries, and conversations with the clergy." It is reported that the latter actively defend their position and adapt themselves to the present-day situation, "for example the priest from Bakht in systematically visiting the nearby villages often helps the fishermen unload their nets, visits their homes on holidays, and has talks with the children." It is reported that a priest in Voronezh province said in a sermon, "Peace will come to earth only when all Soviet people have become Orthodox."

Apart from giving detailed information on the localities studied, these surveys help greatly in understanding the present position of the Party and its agencies on this matter. With all its claim to being scientific and objective, the Party does not seem able to overcome an initial Marxist atheistic assumption in the approach of the surveyors. Thus even facts gathered skillfully, recorded accurately and, it would seem, "without giving offense to the believers," are nevertheless catalogued and utilized primarily for an undisclosed purpose—to eradicate religion. Nevertheless the conclusions of these surveys must be taken seriously when they summarize by saying that there has been a decline in religiosity in the populace as a whole. The reasons are clear: (1) obligatory and, wherever possible, militant atheism on the part of all leaders in society; (2) anti-religious content of formal and informal education; (3) scorn of the clergy as a profession; (4) closing of the majority of the 1917 churches; (5) legal prohibition of any religious activity except worship in registered places; (6) administrative control, de facto amounting to oppression of religion; (7) prohibition of religious "propaganda" which practically eliminates religious literature and use of mass media. One cannot but marvel at the tenacity of religion in light of these negative circumstances.

Having reviewed the status of religion in the broad masses of the people, it is fitting to turn to the developments in government and party policy during the decade. The famous Khrushchev decree of 1954 presaged the new era. A new generation of "godless" had now come of age, succeeding the great pre-revolutionaries, Skvortzof-Stepanov, Jaroslavsky and Lunacharsky. In the universities the psychology of religion achieved recognition, strengthened by the establishment of atheism as a subject for study in the Academy of Science. In the party apparatus, atheism found a champion in Ilichev, head of the Ideological Commission, a man of scholarly bent combined with a crusader's mentality.

In 1959 the Ideological Commission met, worked out a modernized program and policy, and set the whole country going on a vigorous plan to help achieve the purposes of the Twenty-third Party Congress, "communism in this generation," in other words, to overcome religion in the minds and habits of the people by about 1980. There was nothing new in this resolution, except the fresh declaration of intent and a timetable. Certain practical developments, however, inevitably took place, which may or may not be ascribed to the Commission's conclusions. There was an increase of police brutality in dealing with all religions. Even the State Procurator called attention to this, alluding also to cases where local or district courts had condemned and punished religious persons either without just cause or by applying irrelevant laws.

Khrushchev's removal in 1964 was accompanied by a downgrading of the Ideological Commission or, at least, by an attempt to soft-pedal it. In 1966 new legislation appeared which in part stopped some practices on the part of the police and courts, while at the same time it tightened up on other points, chiefly on the production and circulation of typewritten or mimeographed religious documents. Prior to this decade typewriters, mimeographs and even typing paper were seldom found in private hands; evidently improved economic conditions and the abatement of terror have made these facilities to some extent available, even to religion. What has now happened has been a return to the basic Marxist principles of economic determinism, i.e., to expect that a sound economy with social and intellectual satisfactions will eliminate the frustrations which are the cause of religious feelings. By 1980 (or later?) life in the Soviet Union will be of such nature that the roots of religion will have withered.

In the meantime, however, organized religion suffers from the opprobrium of the public and, too often, the depredations of official or quasi-official persons and agencies. To begin with it must be remembered that strict rules govern the registration of local religious societies—parish, congregation, any regular meeting. It is required that not less than twenty local residents in good political standing sign a formal application for such registration; any death or withdrawal must be reported and another candidate presented as a replacement. During the decade under review, many local authorities, evidently under the stimulus of the slogan of "building communism" have used tactical and even illegal means to break up a "twenty", and thereupon close the church. The chief stimulus has evidently come from the Council on Religious Affairs, attached to the Council of Ministers, which up to January, 1966, existed as two councils, one for the Orthodox and one for all other religions. This Council maintains a network corresponding to diocesan and local church organization. Some of the representatives have been quite true to their officially defined task—to see that the laws are kept by both Church and State—but others have been vicious in applying an anti-religious instead of an objective attitude. It should further be noted that not all religious bodies seem to be considered worthy of legalization, usually on grounds of anti-Soviet attitude, public morals or fanatical tendencies. If one is to judge by reports in the Soviet newspapers and other literature, Soviet life spawns many such extremist religions, in all parts of the country.

Here it would be appropriate to deal with the experience of the Russian Orthodox church during the years of 1956 to 1966. When the decade opened, the Church was still basking in the favor which it gained by its loyalty, even heroism, during the great Patriotic War. In 1956 an official delegation of high ranking personalities of the National Council of Churches in the United States spent two weeks in Russia, and in the fall a peer group of churchmen returned the visit. This was not just a visit of courtesy; a program of discussions on agreed topics brought out numerous church similarities and differences. In August, 1956, an even more carefully prepared conference took place in Moscow, between theologians of the Church of England and Russian Orthodox theologians, marking a definite forward step in negotiations between Orthodox and Anglicans.

The high point of Orthodox church status and influence was marked by the Patriarch's speech in the Kremlin in 1959 at a state function for non-governmental and party organizations. In the presence of several hundred topflight personalities, the Patriarch briefly outlined the thousand-year integrated history of Church and State and the contributions of the Church to the welfare of the people of Russia. It was a bold thing to do, and it brought quick reaction. Metropolitan Nikolai of Krutitsk, the next highest ranking person in the Church, was obliged to resign "for ill-health," although he had been the architect of foreign relations for the Church and a pillar in the Party's Peace Movement, which was and still is the chief propaganda instrument of the Soviet state in foreign countries. Also forced to retire was Mr. G. Karpov, head of the Council on Orthodox Church Affairs, a man who had been very fair in handling the operations of the law, even permitting the establishment of ten theological schools.

After this blow, foreign affairs was given over to a thirty-one year old bishop, Nikodim, who at this writing is Metropolitan of the second most important diocese, Leningrad and Nougorod, while continuing as head of the External Relations Commission of the Church. Mr. Karpov's post was given to Mr. Kuroyedoff, whose leadership has been stern and even hostile to the Church. It became the policy of the Patriarchate to replace deceased or resigning bishops with much younger men, with the clear intent of having Soviet-educated men in leadership. Yet on the whole one can say that this plan has not only cancelled out the argument that the Church is a "vestige of the Old Regime," but has stimulated the entry of hundreds of young men into the theological schools and the ministry.

At the same time, whether because of inexperience on the part of the leadership or pressures by the State, the Patriarchate, in 1961, called a Synod which altered the Constitution of the Russian

Orthodox church in a direction which makes it highly vulnerable to secular influence. The chief point was the article which removed the parish rector from a place on the parish council ("twenty") and made him a mere employee charged with sacramental and spiritual functions. Thus the integrality of parish life was destroyed and besides the "twenties" became subject to the whims and even the destructive demands of the representatives of Mr. Kuroyedoff's office, without the trained counsel and spiritual guidance of the priest.

It would seem that this was part and parcel of a grand plan to weaken the Church, while the "person-to-person" anti-evangelism was developed, as reported earlier. The effect of these and other anti-religious tactics has been to close up several thousand Orthodox churches, often for inability to maintain the "twenty", as required by law. Most of the monasteries had long been closed, but now came the turn for the greatest of them, the Kiev Petchersky (caves) monastery, dating from the tenth century. Terrible pressure was also put on the Pochaev monastery through physical persecution of monks and pilgrims, and by 1964 this shrine seemed to be doomed; fortunately a year later pressure slackened.

In the early nineteen-sixties it became known that in Minsk and certain other districts authorities had issued instructions to priests obligating them to refuse baptism to a child unless both parents presented certified signatures of their desire for such baptism. As the sociological surveys have shown, baptism of infants has been a very widespread practice, sometimes done at the request of a grandmother or a sponsor. The new requirement was said to be merely application of the basic law which makes the parents responsible for the child. In practice it has meant that the religious outlook of parents has become publicly known, at a time when religiousness is often used as grounds for discharge from employment.

An extension of the same trend took the form of prohibiting minors from attending worship. Evidently this rule did not apply universally, yet it was indicative of the mood and policy of the Party and government as understood by local authorities. It could have been planned, or possibly it was a case of natural cause and effect, but the nineteen-sixties have seen both a vast reduction in the number of parishes and the closing of theological schools in

Kiev, Lutzk, Minsk and Stavropol. There remain seminaries (undergraduate) at Odessa, Zagorsk and Leningrad, and academies (graduate) at the last two. It may be argued that these schools can train as many priests and theological professors as the Church now requires. Applications are in excess of the capacity to enroll.

In one respect the decade has outshone all others in the life of the Russian Church. This is in its outreach abroad. Even before World War II was over, the Patriarch and other hierarchs began making visits abroad, first of all to the brother ancient Patriarchates of the Near East. In 1948 the Russian Church flatly refused an invitation to attend the founding meeting of the World Council of Churches, but, after numerous feelers and negotiations, plainly for the enlightenment of the state Council on Orthodox Church Affairs, the Church itself and the Western churches, the Moscow Patriarchate applied for and, in 1961, was received into membership in the World Council of Churches. Since then the Patriarchate has deeply ingrained itself in the World Council, with which it now has a senior staff member, in addition to a resident bishop in Geneva as liaison for the Patriarchate.

During these years Moscow has participated and greatly strengthened its position in the counsels of the whole body of Orthodoxy—the four ancient Patriarchates and the ten other national autocephalous or autonomous bodies. The Patriarchate now has exarchs in New York and in London, with scattered parishes in both Western Europe and the Western Hemisphere. Permission has been secured for more Russian monks to go to Mt. Athos, and four have already gone from Moscow.

A continuous program of reciprocal visitations and joint conferences has been developed since 1956. These range as far afield as South India, Ethiopia, Japan and Western Europe. They embrace Orthodox and non-Chalcedonian ancient Eastern Churches, the Lutherans, Methodists, Church of the Brethren, as well as Anglicans. It should be noted, however, that these ecumenical relations abroad are not duplicated by conversations or negotiations with similar church bodies within the confines of the Soviet Union.

If the Catholics in the Soviet Union are seldom mentioned, this is because most of them live isolated in the extreme western part of the Soviet Union, in Lithuania or Latvia, with a few in Byelorussia. What about all the erstwhile Catholics of the Byzantine rite (Uniats) in the Western Ukraine, which in 1939 numbered about four million souls? The full story of 1946 does not belong in this chapter. In that year the Uniats were incorporated into the Patriarchate of the Russian Orthodox church. The latter maintains that this was a "return" of the church forcibly torn from the Patriarchate in 1596, following upon the decisions of the Council of Florence in 1439. There is no clear record of the number of Uniats who may have found their way into the Latin rite churches of the area, nor of the number of former Uniat churches which may now be open and operating under the Orthodox Patriarchate. In any case, one wonders if this situation was not one of the "problems regarding the religious life and the presence of the Catholic church in Soviet territories" to which the communique on the meeting in 1967 of President Podgorny of the Soviet Union with Pope Paul VI referred. The daily *Il Giornale d'Italia* noted the "significance of the encounter . . . we would go so far as to say that if a change in the communist state's attitude on religious questions were to follow upon this meeting, this change might be remembered, be it in Russia or Poland, as the most important historical fact since the war." It remains to be seen.

In Lithuania, and probably elsewhere among Catholics in the Soviet Union, the intensification of atheistic ideological work and similar factors have led to a decrease in the practice of religion. A scientific sociological survey in Panevezhice (Lithuania) revealed that whereas in 1959 seventy-seven percent of infants were baptized, in 1964 only thirty-six percent; in 1959 fifty-six percent of the deceased were buried by the Church; in 1964 only thirty-six percent. In a larger city, Kaunas, the former capital, the drop in baptisms in one year, 1963 to 1964, was from 33.8 percent to twenty-nine percent; of church marriages from 23.9 percent to twelve percent, and of funerals from 31.2 percent to twenty-three percent. In the *kolkhoz* Schwituric, of the eighty-nine families surveyed, thirty-four percent had some member who was a believer. Soviet authors state that the rise in educational and cultural facilities results in a decrease in religious belief and practice. Thus in the Kapsuks region where, in 1960, eighty-nine of 306 students attended church (Roman Catholic), in 1963 only twenty-three of the 314 students did so.

There are few Catholics elsewhere in the Soviet Union, and only six open churches: Leningrad, Moscow, Lvov (two), Odessa and Tibilisi. Thousands of Catholics were either banished or have voluntarily migrated to the East. In such cities as Krasnoyars, in Central Siberia, several thousand are reported to reside, but there is no Catholic church. On the whole the trend seems to be downward for the Catholics as for other confessions. Of the bishops consecrated or authorized by the Vatican, apparently only three in Lithuania and one in Latvia now remain and function.

Special circumstances have affected the experience of the second largest Christian confession in the Soviet Union, those generally termed Baptist, Evangelical, Pentecostal or Adventist. The policy of the Soviet authorities is plainly that of uniting all of these in the All-Union Council of Evangelical Christians-Baptists, as is evident from the secular press and from the reports of the superintendents of this body as they visit the believers in all parts of the country. This policy is resisted by local groups, who sometimes correspond and even meet with like-minded independents, with a view to correlating petitions and plans. Much documentation is now available, of both a secular, that is, Soviet, and religious nature, including copies of some detailed protests and petitions addressed to the All-Union Council or to the civil authorities. As in the case of the forced uniting of the Byzantine rite Catholics (Uniats) with the Orthodox, so with the dissident Protestants. The government holds a whip hand by granting or withholding legalization of the local congregation, which seems generally to be refused unless the group agrees to enter the All-Union Council. No legal grounds for such refusal are to be found in the criminal or civil codes, unless one assumes that the authorities detect disloyal persons or attitudes in the leadership of the dissident "twenties" applying for legalization, and use this as a pretext for refusal. Several court trials, in the course of the nineteen-sixties have claimed to have discovered such disloyalty, and punishment has been severe. The documents reaching the West indicate a good number of such disappointed applicants for legalization, which may mean that delay or refusal is being used as a lever to get the local dissidents to "think it over."

In September, 1966, the All-Union Council of Evangelical Christians-Baptists held a national assembly of delegates from all of its congregations. Some 800 attended, along with foreign guests. Also present were a few delegates of dissident groups. At the close of the assembly it was announced that several of the latter had entered the All-Union Council, but that others were still recalcitrant. No information has yet come regarding the application of an "Organizing Committee" of dissidents for separate legalization, which was made before the assembly, and may still be pending.

On the whole, the Baptist congregations have lost proportionately fewer places of worship than the Orthodox or the Catholics. Furthermore, if we are to judge by their own or the secular press, the religious loyalty of both old and young believers among the Baptists appears to be at a high level, in spite of about equal attention given them by the anti-religious propaganda agencies and the person-to-person workers. This resistance may be accounted for by the fact that the Baptists and the sectarians generally are themselves very missionary-minded. They give much attention to individuals and welcome them emotionally into the fellowship of the group. The congregations seldom have church buildings; usually they meet in homes or in houses externally undistinguishable from other buildings on the street or in the village. This avoids the openness of going to a distinctive church building. For clergy and administrators they depend on acceptance by consensus of members who reveal self-taught knowledge of the Holy Scriptures and a talent for exposition in praying and preaching. Few of the congregations pay salaries to their "presbyters." This is a democratic, spirit-led movement, with the strengths and weaknesses of one depending on the spirit for its preservation and growth rather than on organizational structure and theological content.

It is important to bear in mind that the leaders of the All-Union Council of Evangelical Christians-Baptists are not behind the Orthodox in protesting their loyalty to the socialist cause or participating with the Orthodox in the peace endeavors which conform to Soviet foreign policies. One cannot but accept the voluntariness and sincerity of such loyalty, whether of the rank and file or of the leaders. At the same time there is much evidence that in the congregations of all confessions there are many who have grave doubts about the Christian validity of Marxist doctrine and Soviet reality; they stay in the Church because there they can worship God, but they hold themselves aloof from political expression just as far as possible.

Whether one likes it or not, the non-recognized sects exercise a good deal of influence on party policy regarding religious bodies. This is not because of their size, for neither in local adherents nor as national groups are these sects numerous. Their significance comes from the fact that their extremism and their refusal to join recognized national church bodies draws the ire of the legalistic authorities. The reaction of sectarians to this is to charge the authorities with persecuting them, which further intensifies their fanaticism. Characteristics of these sects are a high degree of emotionalism; uneducated and often unscrupulous, self-aggrandizing leadership; keeping children from state schools; and generally an ingrown, non-cooperative attitude toward the "godless" State. Anti-religious writers publish long articles about them, frequently and unfairly drawing the conclusion that all religion is by nature opposed to enlightenment. Consequently all the churches are tarred with this brush.

Although it has been impossible to cover all aspects of the religious situation in the Soviet Union during this decade—such as theological studies, religious expression after churches are closed, or religion in poetry and literature—perhaps enough information has been given to permit a few concluding paragraphs.

The situation is not all bad. In fact, it can truly be said that the sociological surveys of religion have not only indicated the rise of a rational program as well as a prejudiced ideological approach by the Party; they have provided the churches themselves, whose bishops and leaders read these reports, with data with which to correct, renew and strengthen church life. What is missing is opportunity for the churches to make their own self-studies from a theological angle. This lack of carefully documented, comprehensive information about the Church is one reason, perhaps, for the absence of a Marxist-Christian dialogue in the Soviet Union. During the early years of the regime there were occasional public debates—priest and atheist confronting each other like gladiators —but this practice was soon discontinued. At present, as it has been from the mid-nineteen-twenties, the atheists have full use of publications, films and mass media, while the voice of religion can legally be heard only in places of worship. By way of exception there is a record of a small mixed group of persons in 1965 meeting to discuss religion. In the group were persons representing the press, the schools, the propagandists and the state Council on Religious Affairs, and one Christian, who was a former teacher and a devout Orthodox. One might hope that such meetings may be more frequently arranged, with the participation of men and women of high competence to speak for religion as well as for atheism.

Unfortunately no Soviet people, whether Marxist or Christian, have attended the dialogues arranged by the *Paulus Gesellschaft* in Salzburg, Chiemsee and Marienbad during the last three years. The dialogue between Christians in the Soviet Union, representing and defending socialist society, and Western Christians is carried on through two-way exchanges arranged by certain church bodies in Europe and the United States, also by common participation in the commissions and the general meetings of the World Council of Churches, and in the meetings of the executive bodies and the assemblies of the Christian Peace Conference, whose headquarters are in Prague but whose genesis is in Moscow.

These contacts have reciprocal effect, and are therefore valuable. The West needs to hear from the lips and the consciences of Christians from the Soviet Union explanations as to how they can welcome and support an avowedly atheistic society, one which constantly declares its purpose to transform itself into a Communist society in which, by definition, religion will have no place. What does such a position on the part of Soviet churchmen mean for theology, international affairs, religious education and the cleansing and invigorating of church life in the West? To some extent, delegates from the Soviet Union are able to bring back with them, for limited circulation, not so much bibles and books, but living experience and ideas current in the Western world which they have found compatible with and complementary to their relatively restricted religious outlook.

As far as Western delegates to these gatherings are concerned it is necessary to say that there is always risk of superficial and uncritical acceptance of remarks by delegates from the Soviet Union, failing to take account of the self-limitations imposed on them by the habit of conformity to their government's policies. This is not to say that some of these delegates are not perfectly sincere in their professions of loyalty to their government. What is meant is that in the Soviet Union there is no opportunity in the churches for independent, critical study and discussion on public affairs.

The ideologists of the Party in this decade have shown great interest in Western non-Marxist philosophy and even in definitely Christian theological trends in the realm of sociology, economics, politics and international ethics. Many long articles have been devoted to the Russian philosopher Nicholas Berdyaev, drawing upon his books written and published in Paris as well as upon his pre-Revolution works. There are frequent references and long quotations from Karl Barth, the two Niebuhrs and Tillich. *Questions of Philosophy* ran a ten-page article on the sociological foundations of Martin Luther King. The existentialists, from Kierkegaard to Sartre, seem to greatly intrigue Soviet philosophers. In 1965 and 1966 the "rage" was Pierre Teilhard de Chardin. German neo-Thomism is analyzed in detail. *Pacem in Terris* was widely quoted, and there were several appreciative articles on the Second Vatican Council. Pope John XXIII seemed to be honestly mourned. Pope Paul VI is treated with reserve, which of course is reciprocated by the Vatican. Biblical criticism by German and American theologians and the Dead Sea scrolls constantly recur as evidence that the Holy Scriptures are worthless for the modern man.

It must be noted that these foreign writers, with two or three exceptions, have not been translated so as to make them available for all to read, especially in the churches and theological schools. The original editions in their respective languages are placed on "reserve" shelves, available only to persons accredited by the Party to use them in research. No theologian has access to them.

Even with all this flow of modern, enlightened Christian thought, the leadership of the Party shows no change in its official position on religion. There is constant repetition of the words of Marx, Engels and Lenin, and interpretations of these Communist saints by modern philosophers of the Soviet Academy of Science.

What is at times even more impressive is the comment on religion by simple workmen or *kolkhoz* farmers, quoted in the anti-religious press. There is no question that the atheistic foundations of Marxist communism are deeply embedded in Soviet life. Even the more liberal position on religion taken by the Communist parties in Poland, Italy and France has had no moderating effect on the Soviets. There are occasional moments of relative relaxation, but on the whole both the theory and the practice of militant atheism characterizes the life of both party and government organs and their institutional operations in education and the youth movements. Naturally one wonders whether the 1966 Protocol signed by the Vatican and the Yugoslav government, and the earlier one signed with Hungary, will presage a similar step in Moscow. Favoring it would be certain reciprocal advantages, political and ecclesiastical. The Communist parties in Italy, France and elsewhere would like to think that such a concordat would neutralize Catholic opposition at the polls. On the other hand, with the renewal of direct access and influence on Croatian Catholics granted by the Yugoslav concordat, it may be that the Vatican is stirred with a desire to exercise similar paternal authority and responsibility over the rest of the sixty million Catholics reportedly living in countries under Communist domination. But there are peculiar and historical problems to be met in seeking accord between Moscow and Rome, which are not found, or at least are not so crucial in the other countries. One is Uniatism, which we have already discussed; another is the dynamism of freely operating Christianity which, if given an entering wedge by a concordat, might lead to blunting the edge of atheistic dogmatism, which is the keystone of Marxist communism.

What will then be the future of organized religion in the Soviet Union? The Leninist theory of "communism first in one state" implies the possibility of the Soviet Union establishing such a fair and satisfying society that in Russia the roots of religion would wither, and citizens, being completely free of frustration and need, would have no occasion to turn to God. Yet to this there is the corollary: the "first" such state implies a second, and a third, and so on. In so far as this spreading out fails to happen, in whole or in part, the original proposition loses its validity. Unless communism is established in other countries with the same atheistic presuppositions as in the Soviet Union, the theory of the inevitability and universality of communism will be discounted, and therefore even the communism of the "first" state will remain incomplete. Perhaps, therefore, some religion will in any case continue to exist in Russia, even after achieving near communism, which is its declared objective.

However, Christians must approach the problem from another angle and on a different plane. The Christian concept is that religion is basically not a sociological but a spiritual experience: "My Kingdom is not of this world." The Holy Spirit has acted and will act in any society, regardless of the degree of its scientific, sociological, economic or political perfection. In fact, work for the welfare of human beings is a God-given task on the part of any society, including Soviet society, and this may be part of the reason why churchmen in the Soviet Union can defend their government's policies and practices.

The future of religion in the Soviet Union is thus related to the future of Marxist-Leninist doctrine, and both religion and atheism are influenced by their supporting or hostile movements abroad. Marxism claims to be the civilization of the future, that it will follow capitalism as the latter followed feudalism. Yet the anticipations of the Communist Manifesto of 1848, of the Revolution of 1917, or the Cominform of 1948, have not been realized. Meanwhile both capitalism and communism have modified themselves. Even religion and the churches are going through a period of change. In the circumstances, it rests with Christian believers, with God's help, to take seriously their calling to make themselves and their societies conform so far as possible to the doctrines and traditions of their faith.

# 9

## Soviet Military Policy during
## the Era of Ballistic Missile Defense

### ROBERT D. CRANE

THE PRINCIPAL change in Soviet military policy since the end
of Stalin's rule in the early nineteen-fifties has been a shift in the
basic objectives of Soviet military power. The Stalin era coincided
roughly with a thirty-year period during which Soviet military
power was intended primarily to defend the Soviet Union in case
of capitalist attack on the Russian homeland. After Stalin's death
this basic defensive orientation of Soviet military policy remained
for several years, but the objective became not defense during the
actual waging of war, but the deterrence or prevention of war.

At the end of the nineteen-fifties, deterrence in Soviet military
thought shifted subtly from a defensive to a basically offensive
role. Soviet theorists increasingly believed that a "world socialist
system" had become the dominant force in the world and that it
was gradually encircling the capitalists, despite numerous setbacks
in individual countries. The primary objective of Soviet military
power, therefore, became the deterrence of hostile military responses to the successful expansion of Communist influence and
power throughout the world.

As a result of this basically offensive objective of Soviet military
policy, Soviet foreign policy and military strategy are largely inde-

Robert D. Crane is an independent consultant on Sino-Soviet political
and military affairs.

pendent of developments in American policy and strategy rather than merely reactions to them. Nevertheless the interactions of Soviet and American strategy are becoming increasingly important to Soviet military thinkers. This is particularly true during the modern era when the development of relatively effective ballistic missile defense (BMD) has permitted the Soviets to reemphasize the offensive political objectives of Soviet military power. Estimates of future interactions of American and Soviet strategies have become important in Soviet debates on how much military power is necessary to fulfill both the defensive and offensive objectives of Soviet deterrent policy. In order to understand Soviet military policy during the era of ballistic missile defense it is necessary, therefore, to understand what have been the basic objectives of military strategy in the United States.

During the first decade after World War II, American strategy was designed above all to deter a Soviet attack on Western Europe, because this was considered to be the principal threat to American interests. The United States acquired a strategic offensive force of very modest proportions compared to present standards. Although the American force could not have assured the destruction of Soviet society, it was sufficient for a strategy of "massive retaliation" designed to deter by the magnitude or horror of its threat to Soviet cities.

During the second postwar decade the Soviets broke the virtual monopoly of the United States on strategic offensive forces and threatened the United States with massive retaliation. American strategy therefore was reoriented to deter nuclear war itself, because nuclear war, and not Soviet attack on Western Europe, was thought to be the principal threat to American interests. The United States adopted a strategy of flexible response and controlled war with priority given to "counterforce targeting." This strategy of striking first at the opponent's military forces rather than at his cities was designed to provide the maximum incentive for both sides to terminate a strategic nuclear war if it should break out either by accident or design. It maintained deterrence not through the magnitude of the threatened retaliation, because the credibility of massive retaliation after the Soviets broke the monopoly was no longer high, but rather through the increased likelihood of a limited retaliation to any kind of a Soviet attack on either Europe or the United States. Toward the end of this second postwar decade, the improved intelligence and offensive capabilities on which the "counterforce" strategy was based promised substantially to limit damage to the United States in case the new deterrent strategy failed. The American shift toward a strategy of "controlled war" was followed shortly after the Cuban missile crisis of 1962 by a similar Soviet shift and by limited Soviet support of some arms control concepts to make such a strategy more feasible.[1]

The early years of the third postwar decade, beginning in 1965, brought significant changes into the strategic environment and promised again to change the objectives of American deterrent policy. The first change was caused by the buildup of the Soviet strategic offensive force, which approached parity with the United States in quantity, quality and invulnerability of weapons. This buildup reduced the ability of the United States, which was possibly never great at any time, to limit damage by offensive counterforce weapons. The decreasing vulnerability of the overall Soviet strategic force structure caused the United States to shift its emphasis away from the strategy of "damage limitation." Instead the United States emphasized in its controlled-war strategy the idea of "assured destruction," and relied increasingly on its ultimate threat of massive retaliation against the opponent's entire society.

This new environment reinforced mutual Soviet-American acceptance of the belief, held in the United States long before the Cuban missile crisis, that strategic nuclear war could not serve as a rational instrument of foreign policy and, therefore, that even the offensive psychological exploitation of strategic weapons through nuclear blackmail in crisis situations was not advisable. The result was a permanent American-Soviet détente of varying degrees of hostility. The new environment of near parity in offensive strategic power promoted American acceptance of the belief, long held in the Soviet Union, that the level of applicable offensive force necessary to deter strategic nuclear war is low. The level of applicable

---

[1] *Soviet Nuclear Strategy: A Critical Appraisal,* Robert D. Crane, ed., particularly the sections on "Limited Strategic War" and "Preemption" (Washington, D.C.: The Center for Strategic Studies, August, 1963).

force necessary to deter a strategic nuclear attack was generally considered to be a small fraction of that needed for a "counter-force" strategy of "damage limitation."

The second change in the strategic environment was caused by a continuing shift in international conflict and in military theory away from direct confrontations between the United States and the Soviet Union in favor of indirect conflict in peripheral areas of the world. This was accompanied by a perhaps related shift of emphasis in Soviet thinking, though less so in funding, away from deterrence by retaliatory offense and toward "damage limitation" by active defense. These two changes in the strategic environment required a rethinking of most of the old strategic views on the objects and requirements of deterrence in order to prepare for the strategic environment of the fourth post-war decade beginning in 1975, when the offensive-defensive balance might be reversed. An editor of *The New York Times,* Hanson W. Baldwin, suggested on November 27, 1966, that the change in the strategic environment caused by developments in active defense "is opening a new chapter of technological change that will probably dominate militarily, and to some extent politically, the rest of this century."

The development of functional parity in strategic offensive forces early in the third postwar decade led the two major nuclear powers to accept the existence of a highly stable strategic stalemate. Consequently, they recognized that the problem of "deep-crisis control," and specifically of deterring strategic nuclear attack, had only marginal importance in military and foreign policy planning. The era of nucleophobia, wherein foreign policy is dominated by fear of nuclear war, was over, and a new "post-nucleophobic" era had begun. In Soviet thinking, strategic stability had already been more than adequately achieved and therefore as a problem had become largely irrelevant.

The Soviets were concerned primarily with developing an over-all global and international environment conducive both politically and psychologically to the long-range expansion of their ideas and power throughout the world. Soviet global strategists called fundamentally for a "Marxist" world of conflict between the "progressive" and "reactionary" forces of the world, because they believed that lasting progress was possible only through a dialectical conflict between the two. American global strategists called for a world of order and cooperation, based largely on Christian principles, because they believed that in a stable evolutionary world they could best improve their own society and help other governments reduce or eliminate the social, economic and political causes of nihilistic disintegration and totalitarian revolution. The Soviet strategy called for revolutionary progress through the dialectics of long-range "conflict management" and the American strategy for evolutionary progress through "conflict resolution."

Despite the reduced importance of strategic power for "crisis management," its potential importance for long-range "conflict management" remained. The shift in the basic Soviet deterrence objective from a static and negative goal of war avoidance to a more positive goal of shaping the world environment caused a change both in the mode or mechanism of Soviet deterrence and in the structure of deterrence force required.

During the first "post-nucleophobic" decade, from 1965 to 1975, Soviet strategic power seems no longer to be designed primarily to exert direct "psychopolitical" pressure on an opponent during periods of crisis. During the early "post-nucleophobic" era Soviet power seems intended in large part, if not primarily, to discourage American engagement or commitment, either military or non-military, in areas of high revolutionary potential.

Significant indications of this shift toward a more indirect Soviet global strategy may be found in the proceedings of the Communist summit conference held in April, 1967, at Karlovy Vary. This conference, which ranked officially with the Communist summit conferences of 1957 and 1960,[2] evidenced a new confidence among Soviet military and foreign policy theoreticians. It emphasized the enhanced power of Soviet-bloc military strength and of national liberation wars to bolster isolationist or "peace-loving" tendencies in capitalist countries. This enhanced power, combined with vaunted "contradictions" among the principle capitalist countries, would deter American advisers and decision-makers from even thinking in terms of foreign intervention. The Karlovy Vary conference and the abortive Soviet attempt to orchestrate its Arab

[2] Unsigned editorial, "The Program for the Struggle to Consolidate Peace," *Kommunist,* No. 8 (Moscow, May, 1967), pp. 3-8, 4.

allies before the Near East crisis of mid-1967 indicated an increased importance of local war and hence of "crisis control" in Soviet thinking. Nevertheless the overriding objective of Soviet strategic power during the first "post-nucleophobic" decade seems not to be the creation of a form of extended deterrence, designed primarily to influence the thinking of American decision-makers in times of crisis. Instead Soviet deterrence seems to be designed to control or guide the development of these decision-makers' modes of thought and expectation so that they would avoid the formulation or execution of escalatory responses to Soviet foreign policy initiatives. Even more indirectly, it would be designed to influence over an extended period of time the strategic premises and assumptions of American defense, intellectuals and elite public officials who assist in the formulation of American foreign policy goals. Since it is designed to deter the opponent psychologically from developing or maintaining strategic concepts contrary to one's own strategic interests, this type of deterrence may be termed "psychostrategic deterrence."

The difference between the more traditional type of "in-crisis deterrence" and this "post-nucleophobic" type of deterrence lies most fundamentally in the fact that the former is based on a psychology of direct compellence and the latter on a psychology of indirect inducement.[3] Another important difference between the two is that the "in-crisis" or immediate "pre-crisis deterrence" is effected generally by explicit communication of intent, whereas long-range "psychostrategic deterrence" may well be covert and ambiguous.

At the beginning of the third postwar decade the Soviets had two principal concepts for waging "psychostrategic warfare" against American strategic thinkers. The first was to divert badly needed funds from capital investment, consumer needs and foreign aid to achieve decisive strategic superiority over the United States.

[3] A discussion of both positive and negative incentives in a strategy of "motivational arms control" during the post-nuclear age may be found in "The Strategy of Motivating Peaceful Engagement" in the author's "Some Basic Strategies of Arms Control," *The Prospects for Arms Control,* James E. Dougherty and John F. Lehman, Jr., eds., especially pages 119-122 (New York, New York: MacFadden-Bartell, 1965).

This would stabilize the world in favor of the Soviet Union and encourage American defense and foreign policy advisers to oppose any course of action that might increase tension beween the United States and the Soviet Union. The Soviet Union would then be able to initiate and successfully conclude expansionist, tension-producing moves without effective American opposition.

Soviet strategic superiority could be achieved by a sharp increase in the production of offensive weapons; or it could be achieved by a modest increase in offensive weaponry combined with a sharp increase in the production of active defensive weapons combined with civilian defense evacuation, designed to reduce unilaterally the applicable American offensive deterrent power without a corresponding reduction in similar Soviet power. Exclusive reliance on offensive weapons, however, would contradict the most fundamental tenets of Soviet military thought and also risk an economically burdensome and strategically unrewarding arms race. A strategy of superiority through primary reliance on active defense was doctrinally more feasible, but in other ways perhaps equally unrealistic as a policy choice. Such a strategy might assume a decision by the United States to deny itself an active defense capability in the face of a Soviet BMD (ballistic missile defense) buildup. It might also assume that the rate of development of Soviet BMD technology was already faster than the rate of development of American penetration aids. Reliance by Soviet strategists on these assumptions is improbable.

A second means of waging "psychostrategic warfare" against American strategic thinkers would be to embark gradually on a massive, long-range program of active defense designed to cause a diversion of funds from offensive to defensive power in both the Soviet Union and the United States, sufficient to reduce the applicable deterrent power of both countries. A technological strategy of this nature would necessarily be based on a belief, justified or not, that the rate of development of BMD technology would eventually exceed in "cost-effectiveness" and by other criteria the rate of development in the technology of BMD penetration. Many indications, including the predisposition of many Soviet military theorists to precisely such a belief, made it probable that by 1964 the

Soviets had opted in favor of this second means of "psychostrategic warfare." [4]

The mutual reduction of applicable strategic offensive power by BMD would not reduce the importance of strategic weapons or deterrence in Soviet expansionist strategy. Soviet deterrence strategy, however, would necessarily experience a major change, as described below, in both its object and mode of implementation. Also, in response to this change, the traditional American views on the function of strategic weapons in international affairs might have to be reconsidered.

Probably the principal motivation, though not the only one, for a major shift in Soviet deterrent strategy was the prospect of increased need for Soviet "counterdeterrence" in peripheral conflict situations combined with the prospect of a possibly decreasing Soviet capacity to effect such "counterdeterrence." At the end of the second postwar decade Soviet writings on military philosophy indicated that the Soviets had adopted a strategy of "flexible response" in order to make more credible Soviet intervention or counter-intervention as a deterrent to American direct action in peripheral areas. The abandonment of the incredible Soviet policy of automatic and unlimited escalation in favor of a policy of "flexible response" and "controlled war," however, may have had a result opposite from the one intended, because it indicated that the United States need have less fear of escalation from such direct action. The increased credibility of Soviet action, in effect, may have been more than cancelled out as a deterrent by the decreased danger of escalation.

One way to deter the initial commitment of American military and economic power as a stabilizing force in revolutionary areas of the world would be to increase the credibility of Soviet strategic escalation from an American-Soviet confrontation in these peripheral areas. The most direct way to increase this credibility would be to reduce the damage that the opponent could inflict in a central war. The greater the Soviet capabilities for "damage limitation" by

[4] Robert D. Crane, "Ballistic Missile Defense in the Soviet Philosophy of Strategy," HI-739-DP (Croton-on-Hudson, New York: Hudson Institute, Inc., August 18, 1966), 45 pp., scheduled for publication in *Canadian Slavic Studies,* June, 1968.

BMD the more credible might be Soviet willingness to escalate peripheral conflicts. This greater apparent willingness to escalate would increase the credibility of Soviet intervention or counter-intervention in such conflicts. This, in turn, would enhance perhaps significantly, the Soviet capability to deter any initial American engagement or commitment in areas or situations high in conflict potential.

The choice of this second means of waging "psychostrategic warfare" would clearly not reduce the role of Soviet strategic deterrent force as an instrument of Soviet foreign policy, even though it might reduce the applicable power of Soviet offensive strategic weapons. The objective of Soviet deterrence, however, in one important respect, would have been reversed. The function or objective of Soviet strategic deterrent forces would no longer be the military stabilization of the global strategic environment in order to avoid nuclear war. Rather, these forces would acquire an over-riding political objective of destabilizing the strategic military environment of American-Soviet relations, because for political purposes this environment was already overstabilized. Destabilization of the upper levels of the "conflict spectrum" would be an intermediate goal aimed at the ultimate stabilization of the lower levels in peripheral areas of the world in favor of an expansionist Soviet foreign policy.

The eclipse of nuclear war avoidance as the dominant objective of Soviet deterrence also caused a fundamental change in its mode or mechanism. Soviet deterrence henceforth would be designed primarily to influence the second-order premises and assumptions of the opponent's strategy and foreign policy over an extended period of time, rather than to influence the immediate or first-order decisions of the opponent's political leaders during times of actual tension or crisis. The basic mode of implementation would still be psychological, but it would shift from the "psychopolitical" order to the order of "psychostrategy." The basic goal would be to maintain complete rationality in both fact and appearance and yet sufficient apparent instability at the strategic level, so that the opponent would evaluate the various basic national security policies available to him and select the optimum mix of long-range global strategies on the basis of their contribution to an overall goal of strategic stability.[5] The Soviet hope would be that a heightened concern for strategic stability among Western leaders and electorates would increase Soviet power to deter Western elites from selecting policies and strategies of a dynamic or expansionist nature. This indirect strategy in turn would permit the Communist strategists more safely to maintain or gain the initiative in international affairs.

The adoption of indirect "psychostrategy" as an important, if not the principal, mode or mechanism of Soviet deterrence might require a reevaluation of traditional American views on the function of strategic weapons, and particularly of active defense, in international affairs. First, it might require a reexamination of the force levels required for deterrence. The existence of strategic power no longer would serve merely to influence the thinking of the opponent during periods of crisis. It would now serve also as a subtle instrument of influence and bargaining during times of peace. The primary objective of strategic power would no longer be merely to assure whatever level of deterrence or of "escalation dominance" is considered necessary for the successful management of anticipated or projected crises. Instead the primary objective would be to exploit the "calculus of deterrence" as a constant political or psychological factor in the opponent's mind in order to deter minor political or military actions, far below the maximum level of conflict for which the available strategic power is considered adequate. What might be adequate or reliable deterrence for direct bargaining at a low level of crisis, and minimum or workable deterrence for a higher level of crisis, might be entirely inadequate for indirect "psychostrategic" *bargaining* in a non-crisis situation. If a given amount of deterrent power might suffice to deter an opponent's military action in a serious crisis, an even greater amount of deterrent power might be necessary to influence the thinking of

[5] The concept and nature of basic national security policies (BNSP's) are described in *Notes on the Choice of a Basic National Security Policy,* Carl Dibble *et al.,* HI-684-D (Croton-on-Hudson, New York: Hudson Institute Inc., June 9, 1966). The concept and nature of long-range or environmental global strategies are outlined in "Psychostrategy: A New Concept," in *The Military-Technical Revolution: Its Impact on Strategy and Foreign Policy,* John Erickson, ed., especially pp. 237-238 (New York: Frederick A. Praeger, 1966).

the opponent on possible courses of action of a much less provocative nature during times of peace.

This seeming anomaly is explained by the fact that in the "post-nucleophobic" age the static and negative goal of "crisis control" and war avoidance requires relatively low levels of deterrent force, whereas the promotion of the dynamic and positive goal of long-range conflict management as a means of shaping both the world and the actual or self-perceived role of the opponent in the world, may require the maintenance of deterrent power at much higher levels. The amount of deterrent force needed if this force is to exert a positive or creative influence on international relations may be much more than that needed for the pursuit of a static, status-quo world. Yet the force required for such a creative "psychostrategic" policy may be much less than that required for a static counterforce strategy of offensive "damage limitation."

Second, the adoption of indirect "psychostrategy" by the Soviets would prompt Western strategic thinkers to reexamine the relative importance of the threatened response and the resolve to respond as elements of deterrence. Specifically, the adoption of a general global environment of apparent or even actual strategic instability and intractibility, as an intermediate goal of Soviet deterrence, would require a reexamination of the traditional American views, such as existed, on the role of strategic defense in promoting the resolve to respond and on the stabilizing or destabilizing effects of various combinations of offensive and defensive weapons.

The promotion of mutual disarmament of offensive strategic power through the mutual development of superior BMD technology might be designed to increase the appearance or the fact of instability. This in turn might be viewed as a possible instrument to gain leverage over the most stability-conscious of American strategists. The success of this type of "psychostrategy," however, would depend on the extent of the reduction, if any, of net offensive power, on the degree to which a mutual reduction of offensive strategic power would indeed destabilize the world, and on the degree to which the opponent is motivated by a perception of this destabilization.

The mutual reduction of offensive capabilities might appear to destabilize the strategic environment by making the threat of escalation to strategic nuclear war more credible or thinkable. The removal of the small threat of disaster as a key element of deterrence in favor of a larger apparent threat of moderate damage, however, might have the opposite effect. There is strong evidence that individual criminals are more deterred by high likelihood of moderate punishment than by a small likelihood of the death penalty. Governments seem to react similarly.[6] It is probable therefore that the very appearance of instability at the top of the "conflict spectrum" would provide an additional deterrent to the initiator of a destablilizing chain of action and reaction, and hence would act at every step as a self-deterrent to those who want to pursue a tension-producing policy. Specifically, the heightened effect of self-deterrence against a deliberately destabilizing policy would exert greater deterrent power on a revisionist or revolutionary power like the Soviet Union than on a conservative or evolutionary power like the United States.

Furthermore the mutual reduction of offensive capabilities through the development and deployment of ground-based and space-based BMD and counter-BMD would serve to stabilize the strategic environment by requiring a mutual shift toward relative damage-ratio strategies. A damage-ratio strategy is designed to ensure that neither side would stand to gain in relation to the other, regardless of whether it struck first, either by surprise or in a crisis, or was attacked first, either by surprise or in crisis. The importance of these ratios is seen graphically in the following tables: [7]

When neither side has BMD the premium is on surprise attack even in a crisis. When both sides have BMD neither side can gain relatively from a surprise attack, and it is precisely from a crisis attack that each would stand to lose the most. Mutual BMD, that

[6] See Donald G. Brennan, "Whither Assured Destruction?, and Other Questions of BMD Deployment," HI-722-DP, pp. 6-7 (Croton-on-Hudson, New York: Hudson Institute, Inc., November 4, 1966).

[7] The reasoning behind such ratios is explained in Colonel Richard C. Bowman, U.S.A.F., "Nuclear Strategy and the Arms Race," *Air Force and Space Digest*, April, 1967. Increased damage and injuries from a crisis attack might result from the increased survivability of offensive weapons. Studies at the Hudson Institute, however, indicate that rapid fallout shelter construction by evacuated urban populace might more than compensate for this projected increase in crisis casualties.

## No BMD on Either Side

| | Casualties | |
| --- | --- | --- |
| | U.S. | Soviet |
| I. Surprise, Soviet First Strike | 65% | 25% |
| II. Crisis, Soviet First Strike | 45% | 30% |
| III. Crisis, U.S. First Strike | 30% | 45% |
| IV. Surprise, U.S. First Strike | 25% | 65% |

## BMD on Both Sides

| | Casualties | |
| --- | --- | --- |
| | U.S. | Soviet |
| I. Surprise, Soviet First Strike | 20% | 20% |
| II. Crisis, Soviet First Strike | 30% | 30% |
| III. Crisis, U.S. First Strike | 30% | 30% |
| IV. Surprise, U.S. First Strike | 20% | 20% |

is, possession of substantial BMD capability by each side, would be superior to reliance by one side on assured destruction without BMD, primarily because with mutual BMD the uncertainties, which form a principal element of deterrence in the "post-nucleophobic" world, would be equalized. Without this mutuality the uncertainties would be heavily weighted in favor of the country that had an inherently unknowable defense capability, and against the country that had a certain lack of a defense capability.

Soviet use of BMD to manipulate the opponent's foreign policy premises depends therefore in large measure on the opponent's perception of the real or apparent instability that the Soviets are trying to create. To the extent that Soviet BMD programs are motivated by this type of "psychostrategy," the rationale behind the Soviet BMD programs would be undermined by arguments that a BMD or "reduced-offensive" world should be more stable than one in which both powers remain highly vulnerable to the offensive weapons of the other.

The Soviets probably will continue to press forward with the massive development and deployment of BMD, if only because of a deep-seated dialectical belief that the offensive-defensive imbalance inevitably will be reversed. The United States might respond by announcing a crash program to achieve combined offensive-defensive superiority. This, however, would demonstrate an existing "psychostrategic" vulnerability. The United States could counter Soviet "psychostrategy" more effectively by announcing a more orderly program of BMD development and deployment. Simultaneously, the United States could explain that the American BMD program is designed primarily to revive the prudential policy of "damage limitation" and to increase stability by assuring that under all circumstances the reduction, if any, of applicable offensive power will be reciprocal. This response might avoid a costly and perhaps futile race to maintain the status quo. It might also facilitate the commitment of resources and resolve to meet other problems around the world.

# 10

## A New Russia?

MICHEL GARDER

ALL THE qualified experts are agreed that major changes are taking place in the Soviet Union as it enters its second half century. To many the Soviet Union seems to be in a period of transition between dictatorship and a more representative form of government. However, as the concept of dictatorship does not exactly correspond to the substance of the Stalinist phenomenon it may be more correct to say that the Soviet Union is a materialistic theocracy being affected by a process of laicization.

As a matter of fact, the originality of Soviet communism lies in its religious character. Marxism-Leninism is more than an ideology; it is a religion, however materialistic. It presents the same characteristics as deistic religions, and specifically, of Christianity, of which it is the antithesis.

This religious aspect is to be found in much of the theory of Marx. Engels gave it more emphasis by completing the Communist system with a metaphysical postulate: the material is uncreated . . . it is always in evolution. The logical conclusion of such a postulate was an implicit deification, if not of matter itself, than of the dynamism of matter's evolution. So, even in the nineteenth cen-

Colonel Garder is a former French general staff officer, lecturer in all the French military colleges, adviser for Communist problems at the French Institute for Strategic Studies and deputy chairman of the German Center of Studies for East-West Problems in Munich.

tury, "scientific socialism" was tending toward a type of pantheism and thus was nearly a religion.

A further step was taken by the Russian revolutionaries. Haunted by the example of St. Ignatius Loyola and the Jesuits, Lenin tried to fashion the small Bolshevist party as a "materialistic order of revolutionary knighthood." But the last stage was achieved by the ex-seminarian, Stalin, who, utilizing the embalmed body of his predecessor as a relic, succeeded in eliminating his rivals and erected in the mid-nineteen-thirties a materialistic theocracy in the Soviet Union. This regime was expanded to an empire after World War II due to the complete collapse of Nazi Germany, the heroism of the Red Army and the active help of the Western Allies. Yet this theocracy could not and did not survive the death of the "living god" of world communism. Thus, since 1953 an inexorable sickness, a process of laicization, has affected the very foundations of this religious system, while the empire has been torn apart by schism. The continued survival of a class of "high priests" of the Marxist-Leninist religion is now questionable.

To be convinced that this process is taking place, it is necessary to recall the integral materialistic theocracy that existed on the eve of Stalin's death; to observe the evolution of the Communist world from 1953 to the present; and to examine the actual situation in the Soviet Union today.

Being at the same time the "living god" of dialectical materialism, the "sovereign pontiff" of Marxism-Leninism and the "emperor" of the Communist world, Stalin exerted absolute spiritual and temporal power not only over the Soviet Union but all over Communist countries and parties. This power, reinforced by the existence of an "inquisition"—the political police—found its concrete expression in the "party apparatus," an extraordinary, clerically fashioned administration. Monolithic and hierarchical, this "materialistic clergy" constituted the backbone of the theocracy. At its top, in direct contact with the "divinity" were the "cardinal-satraps" of the Party Presidium who had at their disposal a "general staff" composed of the secretariat of the Central Committee. Under this elite were the "prelate-governors" ruling the various republics, territories, provinces and the three main cities: Moscow,

Leningrad and Kiev, and a multitude of "canons" responsible for the districts. Below these were the "low clergy," officials of local party organizations, and the "activists" or "zealous laymen," ordinary citizens active in party affairs.

Thus the rank and file party members and the non-party citizens —who comprise ninety percent of the population—were cajoled by the "clergy" and its auxiliaries, terrorized by the "inquisition," swamped with propaganda and therefore reduced to the condition of robots working for the glory of an incarnate "historical necessity." The trade unions, the Communist youth and other organizations were the apparatus of the system being utilized by the ruling "clergy" to better control and depersonalize its people and at the same time extend its influence outside the borders of the Communist empire.

In fact, Stalin's cult was not limited to those countries where it was obligatory. In other parts of the world the "missionaries" from the official or the clandestine Communist parties and from crypto-Communist organizations were very active. The myth of Stalin's genius imposed itself so strongly that even today the number of his admirers is much greater in the West than one would believe. This legend was reinforced by the idea that the "historical necessity" which he was supposed to incarnate was working in favor of all the disinherited of the world. To criticize or denounce Stalin was to run the risk of being accused of fascism. It was unbecoming to recall the German-Soviet treaty of 1939 and unseemly to insinuate that the German concentration camps were in a certain respect but a copy of those existing in the Soviet Union.

One can therefore understand that more and more people in the West admitted the inevitability of a Communist victory throughout the entire world. Of course, reinforcing the moral superiority of Marxism-Leninism in these people's minds were the considerable armed forces of the Soviet bloc.

Nevertheless, the real situation of Stalin's empire was not so bright as those resigned to its takeover of the world believed it to be. In spite of the benefits brought by World War II—in particular, Stalin's gains at Yalta and the progress of the French and Italian Communist parties—the "inevitable crisis" had been avoided in the Western states. In the face of the Communist danger most of these countries had joined NATO which was reinforced by American nuclear weapons. The Kremlin could have engaged in, of course, as in the nineteen-twenties, the psychological and political pressure on the colonial and dependent countries. But remembering some previous mishaps in such type of action, Stalin was very reluctant to initiate it. The Communist diversion in Korea in 1950 did not bring him the advantages which he had expected. Only Mao's China gained prestige in this adventure, and this at the expense of Moscow. Not being a man who could admit his own errors, Stalin contented himself with prophesying that sooner or later, "Japan and Germany, as well as France and the United Kingdom, would attempt to free themselves from American leadership, and that their conflicts of interest would multiply." As for himself, he preferred to devote his energy and that of his collaborators to putting his own country in order; for in spite of appearances the internal state of the Soviet Union was far from good.

Besides the terrible loss of life and destruction of property due to World War II, the economy showed the consequences of life in a police state. A significant part of the population was in prison or in labor camps; the rest lived in constant terror of arrest.

Except for heavy industry and the building of armaments, all sectors of the economy were stagnating. This was especially true of agriculture. Immediately after World War II agricultural production was below that of Tsarist Russia in 1913, and this for a population fifty percent larger.

Yet, despite his difficulties, Stalin was still confident in his own infallibility, and at the beginning of 1953 was preparing a new set of purges, which might eventually include some of his closest collaborators.

With the death of Stalin in March, 1953, there began a long period during which the successors of the "living god" struck a series of mortal blows to the theocratic system which they pretended to incarnate. This period of "self-destruction" is still going on. Until now it has taken the form of three stages: the struggle for power, the Khrushchev era, and the ambiguity of the present leadership.

The struggle for power lasted from March, 1953, to June, 1957. During this time the candidates for the Stalinist throne by their continuing competition with one another created a leadership vaccum which worked only to the profit of the Chinese; dismantled the "Inquisition"; made unilateral concessions to their capitalist adversaries; desacralized the very system which they were struggling to uphold; and brought the Stalinist empire close to collapse.

As a matter of fact, by being unable to replace Stalin immediately by a strong, undisputed leader, his successors put Mao Tse-Tung in the position of umpire. He used his influence secretly to support his own candidate: Khrushchev. In June, 1953, all the candidates for leadership did ally against the most dangerous of them: Beria. After that, it is most likely that the fear of one man again gaining control of the state security system led to a partial dismantling of the "Inquisition." Among other things, numerous policemen were dismissed or liquidated; the prerogatives and powers of the chief of state security were limited; the Main Directorate for Concentration Camps was suppressed; amnesties were given to prisoners. Thus one of the pillars of the theocracy was destroyed.

As soon as he became First Secretary of the Party, Khrushchev tended to tighten contacts with the Chinese. In October, 1954, while in Peking he promised Mao "the unconditional support of the Soviet Union for reconquering Formosa, and also the communication to China of all the Soviet nuclear secrets." The other Soviet leaders vainly tried to react, but it was too late. China was near to being the equal of the Soviet Union in the Communist world.

In 1955 the "collegial leadership" tried to placate the Western powers because of the fear which its members felt for American nuclear power. A peace treaty was signed with Austria; Moscow recognized West Germany and German prisoners of war returned home. Khrushchev in particular hoped to obtain from West German Chancellor Adenauer during the latter's visit to the Soviet Union, a promise of German neutrality. As the Chancellor maintained his pro-Western position and West Germany soon joined NATO, the Soviet leaders were finally compelled to a psychological, political countermeasure: the creating of the Warsaw Pact.

Finally, in February, 1956, Khrushchev, trying to put his competitors in a difficult position, launched an attack against the myth of Stalin's infallibility, thus committing, in a sense, an act of "deicide." Being deprived of their "god-figure" the Marxist-Leninist "clergy" attempted to replace him by Lenin. But being dead the latter was not exactly appropriate for such a role. The role of "sovereign pontiff," therefore, for which the competitors were still struggling had become desacralized. As a result of Khrushchev's speech some trouble occurred in certain parts of the Soviet Union. In some places Stalin's statues were decapitated. The unrest then spread to the satellite states, and in August, 1956, disturbances broke out in Poland. In October the Soviet-Polish crisis had become acute, and the Chinese, from their morally strong position, intervened as mediators. The Soviet leaders were compelled to capitulate and sign an agreement with Gomulka, who previously had been in prison for revisionism.

Meanwhile the Hungarians were imitating the Poles. In the face of this new problem the Soviet leaders were at first unable to react. The Chinese intervened again, but in this case they incited Moscow to act vigorously. Taking advantage of the lack of unity between the Western powers because of the Suez Crisis, the Soviet Army intervened brutally in Hungary. The problem was quickly solved, but within the Communist world the real victor appeared to be China. In late December, 1956, Chinese Premier Chou En-Lai carried out in the Soviet Union and Eastern Europe what amounted to a tour of inspection.

As a result of these events the greater part of the Kremlin leaders joined against Khrushchev. The struggle became very intense in the first part of 1957. In June of 1957 Khrushchev found himself in a minority in the Party Presidium, but, betraying once more the ethic of the theocracy, he appealed to the Party's Central Committee, thereby giving power to a body which up to this time had played the role of a shadow parliament. Thus Khrushchev eliminated his competitors as "anti-Party"; the Chinese applauded loudly; and, showing his affection for the victor, Mao himself came to Moscow in October, 1957, to enthrone his candidate.

Khrushchev's reign from June, 1957, to October, 1964, above all constituted a "one man show" in which the actor imagined himself to play the role of "pope-emperor" in a theocracy in which he had previously killed the "divinity"; desacralized the function of "sovereign pontiff"; and sawed the feet off the throne.

Self-confident and unassailable by doubt, Khrushchev would try during his seven years' reign to promote the Soviet economy; to establish on new bases Kremlin hegemony within the Communist world; and to accelerate the global victory of communism over a decadent capitalism. All his efforts were to end as illusions, despite their promising beginnings. The first of these efforts was to play the "pope-emperor." The Chinese, the Albanians, the Roumanians and finally the Soviet citizens themselves successively denounced this posturing, thus prompting Khrushchev's aides to work behind the scenes for his removal. All the other aspects of Khrushchev's activity, whether in domestic affairs or foreign policy, were handicapped by this fault.

The reforms which he undertook such as the decentralization of the economy, the reoganization of agriculture, and reforms of justice, police and education, necessitated an iron fist. Yet with the reforms went a general fall in discipline and other developments which led to confusion and a subsequent weakening of the control of the regime over the population.

As Khrushchev hoped, first of all, to increase his own popularity, and at the same time to prove the superiority of the socialist system through a spectacular development of the Soviet economy, he discovered a number of dilemmas, such as power or prosperity, economic planning or liberalism, autarky or the income of foreign investments, which the dialectic alone could not solve. As it was impossible for him to forswear the religion whose "great priest" he believed himself to be, he was compelled to have recourse to expedients, to improvisations, and to half measures which went against his stated aims.

Presenting himself as the promotor of prosperity, the developer of consumer goods and, consequently, the advocate of disarmament, Khrushchev instead brought about a tremendous increase in Soviet military power without a proportionate increase in the living standard of the population. Thanks to him the Soviet Union's military power could frighten, but its internal economy could not inspire envy. Hitler at least produced cannons in order to seize the butter of other countries; the Soviet arsenal was intended to protect a butter which in the Soviet Union remained an uncommon commodity.

Tempted by the advantages of liberalism, Khrushchev, of course, could not renounce the planned economy. After having supported the necessity of profit incentive and favoring a limited practice of Liberman's thesis, he had been led to strengthen party control over production while at the same time causing discontent among party officials by his reform of the economic administrative structures in November, 1962.

His attempts to obtain increased economic aid from the capitalist states while maintaining autarky resulted in chaos. In the first place, since capitalist states were reluctant to grant long-term loans to the Soviet Union their financial contributions could not represent a real flow of fresh blood into the Soviet economy. The increasing deliveries of industrial equipment coming from outside the Soviet bloc became lost in the Soviet bureaucracy. Complete factories erected by foreign specialists found themselves automatically depreciated as soon as they went into service in the planned economy. Lastly, but possibly most importantly, there was evident bankruptcy in collectivized agriculture. The minor progress shown in comparison with the Stalinist era was mostly a result of increased cultivation in unimportant areas. None of the spectacular Khrushchev initiatives could reach their assigned goals. In 1963 the Soviet Union was compelled to buy corn abroad in order to avoid a serious shortage. With nearly fifty percent of the population working in agriculture this sector of the economy could not feed the rest of the country.

This damaging picture was further aggravated by the consequences within the Communist world of the Moscow-Peking dispute. A major part of the responsibility for this dispute must be borne by Khrushchev himself. Khrushchev, who had been supported by Mao during the struggle for power, had tried since July, 1958, to impose again the leadership of Moscow on the Chinese Party. In 1959 the dispute evolved into a real antagonism as the Soviets decided to use sanctions against their refractory allies with the ceasing of Soviet aid in the nuclear domain. Then in 1960 Soviet economic assistance was cut, and Soviet technicians working in China were called home. In spite of an attempt to solve the problem through an international party conference in November, 1960, the split had become a definite schism by 1963.

Finally, Khrushchev's plan for a new Yalta-type conference aimed at imposing on Western leaders the maximum of concessions on such problems as disarmament and the German problem, and his psychological, political program for the "Third World" of non-aligned nations both failed. Soviet nuclear missiles designed to deter an enemy who had no thought of attacking the Soviet Union constituted in fact an unproductive political weapon. Peaceful co-existence was eating away at the "world revolution." Since the peaceful resolution of the Cuba Crisis in October, 1962, and the signature in August, 1963, of the Moscow Agreement the East-West Cold War had ended without Khrushchev or his aides being completely conscious of this phenomenon. Henceforth, the only real enemy of the Soviet Union was Mao's China, and in this conflict the United States found themselves paradoxically as *de facto* allies of Moscow.

On October 14, 1964, Khrushchev's faithful aides, utilizing the Central Committee, got rid of their chief as if he were a common capitalist prime minister. In so doing they completely finished the desacralization of the highest office in the Soviet Union, sawing off this, the last foot of the throne, for the possession of which they were now condemned to struggle.

The ambiguity of the present leadership has lasted for over three years. Dull and without imagination the hierarchy of the "collegial direction" is vainly trying to deal with all the internal difficulties within the Soviet Union itself and at the same time weather external events. In this respect one can say that their position is very uneasy. As they are the prisoners of their own propaganda, they continue to pretend that they are the champions of "anti-imperialism" at the same time that the religious cold war being led against them by the Chinese is pushing them *nolens volens* to the same position as the United States. But the latter by its involvement in Vietnam is placing the Soviet leaders, who do not wish a new Cuba type crisis, in a more than inconvenient position with their own Communist allies as well as the non-aligned "Third World," where Chinese propaganda is very active.

Moreover, because of their own contradictions, the Soviet lead-

ers are unable to exploit the Chinese internal difficulties. Therefore, the "terrain" chosen by the Maoists for the religious cold
war, revolutionary demogogy, is inconvenient for them.

The only two "victories" which Moscow has won since 1965
over Peking—the Tashkent Agreement and the Tri-continental
Conference in Havana—have both been more profitable to the
United States than to the Soviet Union. In fact, by reconciling the
Indians and the Pakistanis at Tashkent, Mr. Kosygin very much
obliged Washington which was seriously concerned by the India-
Pakistan war. In the same way Mr. Rachidov, in spite of his revolutionary speeches, not only countered the Chinese at the Havana
conference but also partly deprived this conference of its character
as a general "briefing" before large-scale subversive action in all
Latin America.

The only real initiative taken by the Soviet Union since Khrushchev's downfall was the moral backing given to the Arab states
in the Middle East crisis in the spring of 1967. It was an attempt
to meet Chinese accusations of Soviet criminal passivity in the face
of the Vietnam war by putting the United States and the United
Kingdom in a difficult position and thus indirectly helping the
North Vietnamese. In so doing the Soviet leaders were probably
persuaded that neither the Arabs nor the Israelis would initiate a
war. All know what happened. The decisive and swift Israeli victory disturbed completely the Soviet plan. In order to avoid a
direct confrontation with the United States the Soviet leaders were
compelled to give their Arab allies nothing more than moral support and try through secret conversations with the American government to find a compromise. For the Chinese it was a new
occasion for denouncing the collusion between the American imperialists and the Soviet revisionists. In all the revolutionary movements of the "Third World" Soviet prestige was seriously affected.
The Soviet attempt at obtaining a diplomatic success at the United
Nations failed in spite of the presence of Mr. Kosygin himself, and
the Glassboro meeting could but reinforce the Chinese accusations
and make more suspicious of the Soviet Union such revolutionaries as Cuba's Castro.

Even if Soviet influence in the Arab states increased again in the
months following the Middle Eastern war because of renewed mili-

tary aid to Egypt, Syria and Algeria and also because of King Hussein's visit to Moscow, the question is, however, how far this influence might be utilized by the Kremlin for its own interests. It is becoming more and more difficult for the Soviet Union to rearm the Arab states and at the same time preach moderation. With Israeli troops bordering the Nile and occupying Western Jordan tension continues to mount. Chinese propaganda and the example of Castro will certainly find more and more of a hearing among Arab extremists. On the other side Soviet support of the Arabs has mobilized against the Kremlin's position most of the Jews not only in non-Communist countries but also behind the Iron Curtain. It is therefore very difficult to predict what might happen in such a complicated situation. Nevertheless, the fact that all these events nearly coincided with the celebration of the fiftieth anniversary of the Russian Revolution could have but a serious impact on the cohesion of the "collegial direction." Evidence of this has already become apparent.

Nearly fifteen years after Stalin's death one can easily show to what extent the structures of the "materialistic theocracy" have deteriorated. At the top there is a group of "priest-functionaries" of a dead religion—for its divinity has been killed—with a "pope" without a tiara, Brezhnev, and two "co-emperors" without crowns, Kosygin and Podgorny. The former Communist empire has been torn by the Chinese schism and is reduced in fact to the pro-Kremlin faction even within which the primacy of the Soviet Communist party is from time to time contested. Even such a traditional party as the French do not always agree with the Soviet line. The Roumanians permit themselves to scorn the Soviets; the Hungarians are often reluctant to follow them; the Poles seek to play their own game. Even the Cubans now seem to be pursuing their own revolutionary course.

In the whole "Third World" the only client states upon which the Soviet Union can still rely are the socialist Arab states. But one can say that such client states bring about more problems than profits, especially in the political field. The situation is now no longer that of the old Tsarist era when a Russian presence in the Mediterranean would have constituted an important change in the balance of power, or even the situation of the nineteen-fifties when

the Soviet political strategy was aiming to outflank NATO to the
south. As China is now the real enemy of the Soviet Union, the
"collegial direction" could not gain any advantage against this
enemy through a dispersal of its own forces in the Middle East and
North Africa. Actually the Soviet strategists are desperately clutch-
ing at the Arab countries in order to avoid their falling into the
Chinese orbit. Such action is purely defensive and not—as some
people believe it—the beginning of a large offensive maneuver
against the West. On the contrary, the Soviet leaders are to some
extent helping the United States because of the moderating influence they are forced to have on Nasser, Boumedienne and other
revolutionary Arab leaders. The question is how long will they be
able to rearm the Arab states and at the same time prevent the
latter from initiating hostilities against Israel. It is difficult to believe that such a situation could continue indefinitely because on
the one hand there is the growing impatience of the Arabs, and on
the other the Chinese and Cuban propaganda.

All these external problems have, of course, an impact on the
internal situation in the Soviet Union, in which area the "collegial
direction" is facing growing difficulties. First of all, they have to
take into account the younger generation which is better informed
than the older one and which has already figured out the consequences of the bankruptcy of the Marxist-Leninist religion. Propaganda has no more effect on the youth, which is more and more
persuaded of the incapability of the ruling "priests" and of the
obsolete character of the regime which these "priests" are trying to
perpetuate. As the author was once told by a Soviet engineer: "It
is really inefficient to pay well nearly a million sluggards not only
for doing nothing but also for preventing other people from working." For the elite of the country, people such as scientists, technicians, scholars, economists, jurists and agriculturalists, the primacy of the party machinery is no longer justifiable. Having lost
the glory of the leaders of the world revolution, the "priests" of the
dead Marxist-Leninist religion have at the same time proved their
incompetence in the foreign and domestic policies of the Soviet
Union. Even if they are vainly trying to improve the economy by
some "heretical" methods such as Liberman's, they could only

delay a little the moment when their presence at the top would inevitably be questioned.

For many Western experts a new Russia will emerge as a consequence of a long evolutionary process. This means that the present regime will continue while being affected by a series of minor changes leading it almost unconsciously to a state of democracy. In such a concept the Soviet leaders are supposed to be Western-fashioned, lay statesmen trying to find their way through compromises. But Soviet leaders are not lay statesmen, but with the decay of the Marxist-Leninist religion the replacement of the present leadership by lay statesmen is inevitable. Yet due to the political nature of the decaying system the only way for this replacement to come about is through revolution.

At present many factors are coming together that would hasten this revolution. It is, of course, very difficult to predict when and how a revolution could occur in Russia. Yet by taking into account the acceleration of all the historical processes in our changing world one can predict that in five years or so, by the early nineteen-seventies, the theocratic regime might well collapse.

There are, of course, many possibilities. Thus, some people in the West, especially in the United States, assume that the Soviet military leaders will take over. Such an assumption seems unlikely because of the nature of the Soviet armed forces. On the one hand they are completely penetrated by the party apparatus, and on the other hand the best officers are usually excluded from command functions at a high level and are employed in staff or teaching positions. Besides, the troops are draftees and cannot be used as easily as professional soldiers in a military putsch. It is, of course, possible that some units could, in certain circumstances, be used for political purposes, but the army as a whole could never be a revolutionary force.

Although more likely than an army takeover, a popular uprising evolving into a revolution does not seem probable. One can imagine uprisings or insurrections by sectors of the population, but these would be based on social reasons rather than political. The Soviet masses are more concerned with better living standards or a little more freedom than with purely political questions.

A more credible occurrence might be a revolution from above by elements of the managerial class, perhaps in connection with some young *aparatchips* and possibly with the connivance of the political police, the K.G.B. The latter, which has had since 1953 an old count to settle with the party apparatus, might well be helpful for the new forces as other police have been for similar movements in the past.

It would be too long and useless a process to examine all the possible scenarios. The statement of the inevitability of a revolution is a diagnosis, but the nature of this revolution and what could happen afterward, belong to prophecy.

Although civil war and chaos could be possible, it is, nevertheless, hardly credible that a significant part of the population would fight in a civil war for the existing regime. To form a viable government all the revolutionaries would have to do is put into full operation the constitutional structure which already exists and suppress the parasitic organization of the party apparatus. Thus the organization of the State, based on elected soviets, would be revitalized.

After that, of course, the new leaders would have to solve an infinity of problems: nationality questions within the Soviet Union; political, social and economic reforms; foreign policy. However, being free from the restraint of the Party, young, lay leaders would likely be more able to solve these problems than the present ruling "priests."

Within the younger Russian generation, and especially in the technical, scientific and administrative intelligentsia, there are already now enough people who have the statesmanlike qualities lacking in the present leadership. One must hope that they will be able to achieve the change from an archaic communism to a liberal —if perhaps technocratic and socialist—new Russia.

It is obvious that the process of secularization and the collapse of the materialistic theocracy in Russia cannot be isolated from all the other phenomena of our changing world. On the one hand the evolution of the Soviet regime constitutes a very important factor in the changes which are affecting the world as a whole, and on the other hand this evolution is conditioned itself by the changing international situation.

For this reason it is more than difficult to visualize the various versions of a future Russia in an unknown international context. Such questions as the future of China, the outcome of the war in Vietnam, the Middle Eastern situation, possible complications in Latin America, European problems, and, above all, the role which will be played by the United States in the next few years are some of the unknowns.

Nevertheless, if the existing major trends of the present situation are taken to clarify the whole it can be shown that since 1963 the dominant international fact is the antagonism between the Soviet Union and China, even if it is only at the level of a cold war. The United States in spite of the Vietnam war is the de facto ally of the Soviet Union. This de facto alliance is not only based on mutual nuclear deterrence—as some people believe—but also on the fact that the Soviet Union and the United States have a common enemy: revolutionary communism of the Chinese and Cuban kind. As "priests" of the Marxist-Leninist religion, the present Soviet leaders cannot admit that they are in fact the allies of the "American imperialists" and are trying to act as if the Cold War with the United States were still in force. But in fact the Soviet leaders cannot avoid maintaining contact with the United States and in many circumstances acting in connection with the Americans.

One can, therefore, imagine that the new "lay" Russian leaders when they came to power would be led by the dynamic of the present situation to become de jure allies not only of the United States but also of the other Western countries due to the dangers which might occur from revolutionary communism in the non-aligned Third World.

Personally, this author believes that the coming Russian revolution would be a great step in the direction of a unification of all the Northern Hemisphere in order to solve by common effort the problems which are being posed by the underdeveloped Southern Hemisphere.

# General Bibliography

Billington, James H. *The Icon and the Axe: An Interpretative History of Russian Culture.* New York: Knopf, 1966.

Hazard, John N. *The Soviet System of Government.* (rev. ed.) University of Chicago Press, 1964.

Lowenthal, Richard. *World Communism: The Disintegration of a Secular Faith.* New York: Oxford University Press, 1964.

Meyer, Alfred. *Communism.* (3rd ed.) New York: Random House, 1967.

Salisbury, Harrison (ed.). *The Soviet Union: The Fifty Years.* New York: Harcourt, Brace and World, 1967.

Schapiro, Leonard. *The Communist Party of the Soviet Union.* New York: Random House, 1962.

Toynbee, Arnold J. and others. *The Impact of the Russian Revolution.* New York: Oxford University Press, 1967.

Treadgold, Donald. *Twentieth Century Russia.* Chicago: Rand McNally, 1964.

# Specialized Bibliography

CHAPTER 1

Barghoorn, Frederick. *Politics in the USSR.* Boston: Little, Brown & Co., 1966.

Fainsod, Merle, *How Russia Is Ruled.* (rev. ed.) Cambridge: Harvard University Press, 1963.

Gripp, Richard. *Patterns of Soviet Politics.* (rev. ed.) Homewood, Illinois: Dorsey, 1967.

Linden, Carl. *Khrushchev and the Soviet Leadership, 1957-1964.* Baltimore: Johns Hopkins, 1966.

Meyer, Alfred. *The Soviet Political System, An Interpretation.* New York: Random House, 1965.


CHAPTER 2

Bornstein, M. and Fusfeld, D. (eds.). *The Soviet Economy: A Book of Readings.* (rev. ed.) Homewood, Illinois: Irwin, 1966.

Campbell, R. W. *Soviet Economic Power.* (2nd ed.) Boston: Houghton Mifflin, 1966.

Dobb, M. *Soviet Economic Development Since 1917.* (rev. ed.) New York: International Publishers, 1966.

Nove, Alec. *The Soviet Economy.* (rev. ed.) New York: Praeger, 1965.

Spulber, Nicolas. *The Soviet Economy: Structure, Principles, Problems.* New York: Norton, 1962.

CHAPTER 3

Belov, Fedor. *The History of a Soviet Collective Farm.* New York: Praeger, 1955.

Jasny, Naum. *Khrushchev's Crop Policy.* Glasgow: George Outram & Co., 1965.

Karcz, Jerzy (ed.). *Soviet and East European Agriculture.* University of California Press, 1967.

Laird, Roy. *Collective Farming in Russia.* Lawrence, Kansas: University of Kansas Press, 1958.

Laird; Sharp; Sturtevant. *The Rise and Fall of the M.T.S. as an Instrument of Soviet Rule.* Lawrence, Kansas: University of Kansas Press, 1960.

Laird, Roy (ed.). *Soviet Agricultural and Peasant Affairs.* Lawrence, Kansas: University of Kansas Press, 1963.

Mitrany, David. *Marx Against the Peasant.* London: George Weidenfeld and Nicholson, Ltd., 1951.


CHAPTER 4

Cornell, Richard. *Youth and Communism: An Historical Analysis of International Communist Youth Movements.* New York: Walker, 1965.

Fisher, Ralph T., Jr. *Pattern for Soviet Youth: A Study of the Congresses of the Komsomol, 1918-1954.* New York: Columbia University Press, 1959.

Kassof, Allen. *The Soviet Youth Program: Regimentation and Rebellion.* Cambridge: Harvard University Press, 1965.


CHAPTER 5

Bereday, George; Brickman; Read (eds.). *The Changing Soviet School.* Boston: Houghton Mifflin, 1960.

Bereday, George; Pennar; Jaan (eds.). *The Politics of Soviet Education.* New York: Praeger, 1960.

Bowen, James. *Soviet Education: Anton Makarenko and the Years of Experiment.* Madison: University of Wisconsin Press, 1962.

Counts, George. *The Challenge of Soviet Education.* New York: McGraw-Hill, 1947.

DeWitt, Nicholas. *Education and Professional Employment in the USSR.* Washington: National Science Foundation, 1961.

————. *Soviet Professional Manpower: Its Education, Training, and Supply.* Washington: National Science Foundation, 1955.

Hans, Nicholas. *The Russian Tradition in Education.* London: Routledge and Kegan Paul, 1963.

King, Edmund (ed.). *Communist Education.* Indianapolis: Bobbs-Merrill, 1963.

Trace, Arthur. *What Ivan Knows That Johnny Doesn't: A Comparison of Soviet and American School Problems.* New York: Random House, 1961.

CHAPTER 6

Bochenski, J. M. *Soviet Russian Dialectical Materialism.* Dordrecht: D. Reidel Publishers, 1963.

Chambre, Henri, S.J. *From Karl Marx to Mao Tse-Tung: A Systematic Survey of Marxism-Leninism.* New York: P. J. Kenedy & Sons, 1963.

De George, Richard T. *Patterns of Soviet Thought.* Ann Arbor: University of Michigan, 1966.

Edie; Scanlan; Zeldin; Kline (eds.). *Russian Philosophy.* 3 vols. Chicago: Quadrangle Books, 1965.

*Soviet Studies in Philosophy.* A journal of translations from original Soviet sources published by the International Arts and Sciences Press, New York.

*Studies in Soviet Thought.* A Quarterly Review of Philosophy in Eastern Europe of the Institute of East-European Studies at the University of Fribourg, Switzerland.

Wetter, Gustav. *Dialectical Materialism: A Historical and Systematic Survey of Philosophy in the Soviet Union.* New York: Praeger, 1959.

CHAPTER 7

Alexandrova, Vera. *A History of Soviet Literature, 1917-1964: From Gorky to Solzhenitsyn.* Garden City: Doubleday, 1964.

Brown, Edward J. *Russian Literature since the Revolution.* New York: Collier, 1963.

Hayward, Max (ed.). *On Trial: The Soviet State Versus 'Abram Tertz' and 'Nikolai Arzhak.'* New York: Harper & Row, 1966.

Johnson, Priscilla and Labedz, Leopold (eds.). *Khrushchev and the Arts: The Politics of Soviet Culture, 1962-1964.* Cambridge: MIT Press, 1965.

Swayze, Harold. *Political Control of Literature in the USSR, 1946-1959.* Cambridge: Harvard University Press, 1962.

CHAPTER 8

Bourdeaux, Michael. *Opium of the People: The Christian Religion in the USSR.* Indianapolis: Bobbs-Merrill, 1966.

Cizek, Walter J., S.J., with Daniel L. Flaherty, S.J. *With God in Russia.* New York: McGraw-Hill, 1964.

Fletcher, William. *A Study in Survival.* New York: Macmillan, 1965.

Fletcher, William and Stover, Anthony (eds.). *Religion and the Search for New Ideals in the USSR.* New York: Praeger, 1967.

Kolarz, Walter. *Religion in the Soviet Union.* New York: St. Martin's Press, 1961.

Pollock, J. C. *The Faith of the Russian Evangelicals.* New York: McGraw-Hill, 1964.

Stroyen, William B. *Communist Russia and the Russian Orthodox Church 1943-1962.* Washington: Catholic University of American Press, 1967.

Struve, Nikita. *Christians in Contemporary Russia.* New York: Charles Scribner's Sons, 1967.

Wetter, Gustav A., S.J. *Soviet Ideology Today.* New York: Praeger, 1962.

Zernov, Nicolas. *The Russian Religious Renaissance of the Twentieth Century.* London: Darton, Longman & Todd, 1963.

CHAPTER 9

Beaufre, Andre. *An Introduction to Strategy.* New York: Praeger, 1965.

Bloomfield, Lincoln P., Clemens, Walter C., Jr. and Griffiths, Franklyn. *Khrushchev and the Arms Race: Soviet Interests in Arms Control and Disarmament, 1954-1964.* Cambridge: MIT Press, 1966.

Crane, Robert D. (ed.). *Soviet Nuclear Strategy: A Critical Appraisal.* Washington: The Center for Strategic Studies, Georgetown University, 1963.

Dallin, Alexander, *et al. The Soviet Union, Arms Control and Disarmament, A Study of Soviet Attitudes.* New York: School of International Affairs, Columbia University.

Dougherty, James E. and Lehman, John F., Jr. (eds.). *The Prospects for Arms Control.* New York: Macfadden-Bartell, 1965.

Erickson, John (ed.) *The Military-Technical Revolution: Its Impact on Strategy and Foreign Policy.* New York: Praeger, 1966.

Erickson, John. *The Soviet High Command: A Military-Political History, 1918-1941.* New York: St. Martin's Press, 1962.

Garder, Michel. *A History of the Soviet Army.* New York: Praeger, 1966.

Garthoff, Raymond L. (ed.) *Sino-Soviet Military Relations.* New York: Praeger, 1966.

Garthoff, Raymond L. *Soviet Military Policy: A Historical Analysis.* New York: Praeger, 1966.

Horelick, Arnold L. and Rush, Myron. *Strategic Power and Soviet Foreign Policy.* Chicago: University of Chicago Press, 1966.

Kintner, William R. *Peace and the Strategy Conflict, 1967.* New York: Praeger, 1967.

Kolkowicz, Roman. *The Soviet Military and the Communist Party.* Princeton: Princeton University Press, 1967.

Strausz-Hupe, Robert, Kintner, William R., Dougherty, James E. and Cottrell, Alvin J. *Protracted Conflict.* New York: Harper and Brothers, 1959.

Wolfe, Thomas W. *Soviet Strategy at the Crossroads.* Cambridge: Harvard University Press, 1964.

CHAPTER 10

Deutscher, Isaac. *The Unfinished Revolution: 1917-1967*. New York: Oxford University Press, 1967.

Garder, Michel. *L'Agonie du regime en Russie sovietique*. Paris: La Table Ronde, 1965.

# Index